THE
9th Colony
HORNET'S NEST

Colin Curtis

The 9th Colony - Hornet's Nest

Copyright © 2024 by Colin Curtis

All rights reserved. No part of this book may be reproduced or transmitted in any form or by any means, electronic or mechanical, including photocopying, recording, or by any information storage and retrieval system, without written permission from the publisher.

ISBN: 979-8-8693-8311-2 (Paperback)
ISBN: 979-8-8693-8312-9 (Hardcover)
ISBN: 979-8-8693-8310-5 (eBook)

Contents

1. An Unexpected Encouter..................................8
2. Enforced Captivity.....................................24
3. Joining the Resistance.................................37
4. The Calm before the Storm..............................49
5. Fleeing for Their Lives................................59
6. Seeking Sanctuary......................................69
7. The Reunion..80
8. A Katarian Encounter...................................92
9. Let the Battle Commence...............................104
10. Repercussions of Infidelity..........................116
11. The Battle for Lunaria..............................125
12. A Hollow Victory....................................137
13. The Journey Home....................................147
14. Forming a Planetary Alliance........................157
15. The Final Conflict..................................169

1

An Unexpected Encounter

Simon and Alex drove through the countryside in the quiet backwater county of Hertfordshire in England. As they drove to the top of the hill, high in the tree line, they looked down towards a dilapidated barn that they had been working on in a clearing about five hundred yards ahead of them. Several minutes later they pulled up into the car park just Infront of the barn conversion. Simon a twenty-eight-year-old decorator, stepped out of the vehicle. He was quite well built with grey hair, which was unusual for a man of his age. As a child he'd suffered with alopecia, which left him with no hair for several years and when it eventually grew back, the color pigment had been destroyed, so it grew back grey. He was a very hard worker and had a reputation for always getting the job done on time. He normally worked as a foreman running jobs with dozens of employees underneath him, but on this occasion, he was working directly on the tools with his best mate Alex. As they began to unload some tools from the van, a huge shadow appeared above them, instantly blocking out the sunlight. They naturally looked up and were shocked and in awe at what they saw. A craft was circling above them, just out of reach. It was approximately thirty feet in diameter, black in color, and circular in design. It made no sound. In fact, everything around it also fell into a deafening and eerie silence. It was almost like time itself had stood still!

Simon was the first to attempt to touch it, without too much success. Still, it just hovered there, as if it were waiting for something, or maybe it was just observing them.

Inquisitive as Simon was, he felt compelled to find out more about this strange object. He was a character who was very much into his sci-fi, and to him, this was something that he just couldn't possibly resist. To miss out on an opportunity like this, would be something that would haunt him for the rest of his days!

Still in awe, he picked up the nearest thing to him, which happened to be a small stone, and he threw it at the craft. The stone disintegrated several inches before it made contact, much to Simon and Alex's astonishment.

"Did you see that?" asked Simon, brimming with excitement.

"Yes ... and I think it's probably not a good idea to do it again!" Alex replied nervously.

"Why not? Nothing happened the first time, did it?"

"Yeah, but—"

Before Alex could finish his sentence, Simon had already picked up another stone and taken aim at the craft, but this time before he could release it, a beam of light shot towards him and disintegrated it, scorching his right hand.

Clearly this sudden action had put the fear of god into Alex, and Simon looked on anxiously as his friend immediately dived for cover to avoid being attacked himself. There was a moment's silence before the craft rose in height by several feet.

On seeing this, Alex took his opportunity and crawled over to his friend to check up on his condition.

"Are you OK? How badly hurt are you?" he asked.

"I'm OK! Don't worry; it just burnt my hand a little—that's all. Aside from the stinging sensation, I feel quite elated! Really, don't worry. This is the best thing that's ever happened to me!"

While Simon and Alex were discussing what to do next, something was happening above them. Several slots were opening on the undercarriage of the ship, and what could only be described as a hollow rectangular cage was being lowered from them. A clunking noise was heard as it locked into position, and the craft then reduced altitude to its original height. This time, though, it was within reach, due to the cage that suspended underneath it. Simon had now regained his focus, and without fear, he walked towards it.

"What the hell are you are doing? We need to get the fuck out of here!" Alex screamed.

"I need to see what it is."

"Are you mad? This thing's likely to kill you!"

"Look—I may never get the chance to do this again! OK?"

"You're off your rocker, mate; it's already attacked you once and burnt your hand as a result. Think about what you're doing," Alex pleaded.

"Don't worry. It was just defending itself. That means it's intelligent. I'm sure with that kind of technology, that it could have done far worse if that was its intention."

"I still think that we should leave it well alone."

"Well, I don't, so we'll just have to agree to disagree," said Simon stubbornly.

With that, he walked straight towards the craft, totally ignoring his friend's advice, and grabbed hold of the suspended cage. Alex just stood back, cowering in the doorway of the barn, too frightened to join his mate.

Simon pulled himself into the inside of the framework of the cage. From there he could touch the surface of the black hovering disc. "It's OK! It feels kind of warm and it's vibrating slightly, but aside from that it's fine. Come up and see for yourself."

Alex reluctantly approached the cage and reached up to grab hold of it. As he did, a flash of light propelled him to the ground. At the same time a translucent blue light surrounded and engulfed the cage, trapping Simon inside.

"Alex! Alex, are you OK?" Simon shouted.

"It's OK; I'm all right, just a little dazed—that's all. You need to get the hell out of there right now!" Alex replied.

But Simon was going nowhere fast. The surrounding blue light was some sort of force field, and although he could see through it, he couldn't penetrate or pass through it.

"I can't get out!" he shouted back, sounding very concerned.

"I fucking knew it! I told you not to touch, but as usual you didn't listen. Look don't panic. OK? Are there any buttons or anything that you can see that might release you?

A loud buzzing noise started coming from the cage, and the next thing that Simon saw was a panel materializing in front of him. It was the first sign of gadgetry that he had seen, and like the craft, it was also black and smooth in design. In the center of the panel were two shallow eight-inch holes, and inside each of them he could clearly see a leaver.

Being curious and with little other options, he reached into one of the holes and grabbed the leaver, which turned in an anti-clockwise direction. Nothing happened, and as he let go, the leaver sprang back into its original position. He then repeated his actions with the other hole, and much to his annoyance it did the same.

"Try turning them both at the same time," Alex suggested.

"OK, hang on."

As the leavers clicked into position, a high-pitched noise could be heard, and the cage began to fill up with a luminous orange liquid. Panic set in as Simon desperately tried to reverse his actions.

"I can't get out! I can't get out!" he screamed, frantically banging his fist against the surrounding force field.

Simon looked on as Alex picked up a hammer from his tool bag and ran towards the cage in a vain effort to release his friend, but before he could reach him the craft rose ten feet into the air.

He could do little but watch as the rest of the cage filled up with the liquid, slowly engulfing Simon.

In an instinctual reaction, Alex threw the hammer at the cage. Predictively, though, it disintegrated just like the stone. The difference this time, though, was self-evident, as the craft immediately attacked, shooting beams of light directly at Alex.

In the final seconds of consciousness Simon looked on as his friend was cut to pieces by the beams of light and collapsed lifelessly on the dusty ground.

Simon retched as he swallowed the fluid, until he was silent, his body no longer moving.

* * *

Several months later, onboard the saucer ship that had captured Simon, a beeping sound is heard coming from one of the many chambers on board.

Inside the room, stacked vertically, there were a dozen cryogenic tubes lined up side-by-side, with tubing attachments and digital monitoring screens surrounding them.

The third cryo tube along was malfunctioning, and the viewing panel suddenly unlocked itself, opening prematurely, revealing a human woman, who was now beginning to come around from her long-induced sleep.

It took around ten minutes before she was conscious enough to be able to move her arms and muster up enough strength to break free from her restraints and climb out of the tube that she'd been placed in.

The woman fell to her knees, and with her palms flat down on the hard clean surface, she lifted her head. As she opened her eyes, she slowly began to regain her focus, as she scanned the room to take in her surroundings. Eventually she mustered up enough strength to stand up, still unsure of where she was or what the hell was going on, she began to wander around this strange area that she now found herself in.

She walked along the poorly lit corridor and came across a second room, where she discovered another six cryogenic tubes. They were much larger than the ones she had just climbed out of. Inside these tubes, she could just about make out much larger human like forms, and she assumed that these were more likely to be her captors.

At this point, she decided that there would be safety in numbers, so she returned to the original room where she had first awoken.

One by one, she managed to disable and open the remaining eleven cryo tubes containing the other abducted humans. Most of them awoke frightened and confused as they regained consciousness, apart from one guy who seemed full of confidence and at ease with the situation.

"Hi... I'm Simon... thanks for releasing me, tell me what you know so far," he said confidently.

"Hey Simon...I'm Elle, but you can call me El. Like you I woke up here on this ship, I believe we are in space, and looking out into the void of darkness outside, there doesn't seem to be any sign of Earth. There are several rooms like this one with humans inside, but the cryogenic tubes in the room next door are much larger. The people that are frozen inside these ones are not like us," said Elle.

"What do you mean? ... are they little green men?" Simon asked.

Elle laughed... "no they not green and definitely not little," she replied

Simon and Elle slowly walked up the corridor to explore more of the vessel, and eventually found themselves in the control room with an oversized chair, that was situated in front of a large control panel with several monitors displaying strange symbols. Fortunately, there didn't seem to be any conscious crew members on board, and once Simon had familiarized himself with the general layout of the vessel, he followed Elle into the other cryo room, to see these aliens for himself.

"Well... they're certainly not little, but if we are going to take control of this ship, then I'm afraid we're going to have to revive one of them as the controls on this ship are in a language that I can't understand."

Elle told Simon that she had been abducted whilst on maneuvers with the military. She was a trained soldier that had seen several conflicts. Protocol for releasing prisoners would be to tie them up first and bearing in mind that this alien was around eight foot tall and built like the hulk, it was probably the best thing to do.

"It might seem a little brutal, but I think we should also execute the rest of the crew," said Simon. "As they would most certainly overpower us if they got free."

After returning to the original room, Simon asked everyone to search around to see if they could find anything that they could use as a weapon, and once they'd discovered the armory, they returned to the room with the aliens in, and opened the pods one by one, shooting the aliens in the head until there was only one left.

The sixth and final crew member was then tied up with some wire that Elle had found in her search of the ship, and as he became conscious, he quickly realized his predicament, and suffice to say he wasn't a happy bunny!

Simon and Elle escorted him into the control room and sat him down in front of the monitors. Simon prodded him aggressively and pointed to the controls, shouting at him to unlock them from the auto pilot that they were set on.

The giant of a man looked straight at Simon and just cussed at him in some strange language. With that Simon asked two of the other abductees to restrain him, and he began to repeatedly hit him in the face, while screaming at him to give him control of the ship. At this point Elle came over a little dizzy and decided to lay down for a bit to catch her breath.

"Ok ok! ... I will give you control of the ship, if you agree to free me once we land" said the giant who was now speaking the kings English as clearly as Simon.

Simon was quite surprised at what he was hearing. "So... you know our language then." Snapped Simon, "you've obviously been doing this for some time,"

"Not at all... this devise around my neck translates the sounds I hear and the words I speak into many languages."

"Who are you? And why have you abducted us?" Simon demanded to know.

"We are the Mycien, and I will never give you control of this vessel!" he screamed as he hit the control panel.

The ship jolted into action and began to move at speed towards a nearby planet.

Suddenly in all the confusion, the Mycien crew member managed to break free from his restraints, and he struck out at one of the humans that were holding him, knocking him to the floor. It didn't take him too long to overpower the other guard before turning his attention to Simon.

"Now it's your turn to die little man," he said as he grabbed Simon around the throat and lifted him off the floor.   Luckily for Simon though his escape was short lived, as Elle re-entered the room and shot him in the back of the head.

The blood and pieces of his brain splattered across Simon's face, and as the Mycien released his grip on him, he collapsed on the floor.

"Ahhhh!" .... Simon blurted out as he pulled the chunks of Mycien flesh off him.

With his heart pounding, and his breathing still a little erratic, due to the adrenalin pumping inside of him, Simon looked up towards Elle, and with a sigh of relief, he nodded towards her to thank her for her timely intervention.

Elle smiled and walked over to Simon; she stretched out a hand to pull him up off the floor. As she did so, he stood up and stumbled into her arms. For a brief moment, they both forgot about the situation that they were in, and as their eyes fixed on each other, Elle felt an overwhelming urge to kiss him, but before she could act on her desire, one of the other humans interrupted their moment of passion.

"I hate to disturb you two love birds, but I think we are going to crash into that planet over there."

Simon jumped onto the pilots chair and tried in vain to take control of the ship, but it wasn't playing ball.

"Give me the gun," Simon screamed.

He took aim and fired off several shots at the control panel, and the ship suddenly began to slow down, veering off the course that it was on.

Slowly it went into a landing sequence, and it eventually landed, dropping them into a clearing in the Forrest below. Surprisingly though, they had a relatively soft landing, with the craft stopping just short of the ground, and as the engine noises shut down a flashing light appeared on the now damaged control panel.

"What's that?" asked Elle.

"How the hell would I know?... Let's push it and find out," said Simon.

After a few seconds a clunking noise could be heard, and the feet of the flying saucer embedded themselves in the ground.

"Ok... we'd better not waste any time, I want everyone to search the ship fully to see if there's anything that we can use like food, water, or first aid etc.'

Simon joined the others in the search, and as he went into the back room of the ship, he noticed what looked like a hidden panel in the wall. He looked around and picked up a leaver to try and prize the panel free.

The panel opened, and inside was a coffin like container with a girl inside, submerged in a white liquid.

Simon pulled the coffin out of the compartment in the wall and reached down into the liquid to lift the girl out, and he laid her on the ground. She wasn't breathing... her mouth and throat were still full of the white liquid.

Simon shouted for help and began clearing her airways before trying to resuscitate her by breathing into her lifeless body and applying chest compressions.

After what seemed like an eternity the girl retched and spat out the remaining liquid from her lungs, and for a brief moment, she regained consciousness and opened her eyes.

To Simons amazement, her eyes were yellow, and she stared straight at Simon whose gaze was now firmly transfixed on this strange looking girl... seconds later she closed her eyes and fell back into a state of unconsciousness....

Simon repeatedly tried in vain to wake her from her coma, but to no avail. Finally, he picked her up and carried her into one of the accommodation chambers at the rear of the ship.

Simon instructed one of the female abductees to watch over her, and to inform him if there was any change.

He then left the room and made his way back to the control room, passing two other rooms with various devices inside, and removed the translation device and a digital wrist bracelet from the dead Mycien crew member, and put them on himself.

Amazingly, as he looked at the control panel, the basic commands now made sense to him, although after pressing a few options, it quickly became apparent that there was a major fault on the ignition sequence. It was probably down to the fact that he'd taken several pot shots at it will they were still in space.

Simon decided to go back and check up on the mysterious girl he'd found earlier, and as he passed the first of the two rooms he glanced inside and couldn't believe his luck. On the wall above the machines in the room was a sign saying food replicator.

"Would you look at that!... must be our lucky day" said Simon to Elle, who had just appeared at the doorway

"What? What have you found" asked Elle.

"It's our life saver... they are food and drink replicators.

"That's great news, and apart from a selection of gadgets and toys that we've come across, I believe the room next door is full of medical equipment, although I can't work out what's what. I'm going to need your newly acquired translation skills" said Elle smiling.

"It good to see you smile Elle, let's hope that smile stays on your face as we progress here in this strange world that we now find ourselves in"

Among the abducted humans were several medical staff, which Simon took full advantage of, and once they'd worked out how the medical machines worked, they hooked them up to the girl in the coma, so that they could monitor her heartbeat, and make sure her stats didn't deteriorate.

There was very little else that Simon could do for her right now, so he turned his attention to the situation they now found themselves in.

He and Elle stepped outside onto the soft grassy meadow that covered the clearing in the center of the forest that they'd landed in. To the right of the clearing was a gap in the trees, where a small dirt trail, no wider than a medium sized van led off into the dense forest that surrounded them.

The air was quite breathable, and the temperature was similar to a warm summer's day, although, it was clear that the light was fading fast. The planet wasn't that dissimilar from Earth, apart from its inhabitants and of course its technology.

As well as the translation device, Simon also had this bracelet on his wrist, and he decided that now was as good a time as any to give it a try.

"Ok ... Firstly, we need to build a fire, and everyone that's not doing anything right now can start by gathering wood," said Simon

Elle wasted no time in assuming the role of second in command, and began organizing teams of people to gather and sort out the timber for the fire.

Simon pressed one of the buttons on his wrist bracelet, and a humming noise started emanating from the ship.

Moments later the vast ship that had stood in front of him, suddenly disappeared.

Simon walked forward and cried out loud, as he bent his hand back when it made contact with the invisible ship.

"OMG ... it's like the cloak of invisibility from the harry potter story, only on a much larger scale" said Simon jokingly.

Elle was equally impressed and asked if he could make it reappear just as quickly, and much to her surprise by pressing another button that's exactly what he did.

In the middle of the bracelet there was a small circular disc, this could be rotated both in a clockwise and anti-clockwise direction, and after playing around with the bracelet, Simon soon realized that if he turned the disc while the invisible shield was activated, then the gap in the forest also disappeared, giving the illusion that it wasn't even there. This was true from whichever side of the force shield you were standing on.

"Wow!... now that's impressive, and it means that we can mask our presence here from onlooking eyes.

"It seems that we have landed in the perfect position to set up base camp," said Elle.

Among the other smaller gadgets that Elle's search team had come across on the ship, were a set of communication and tracking devices that were locked to the ship's frequencies. These devises would be helpful in finding their way back to the campsite when leaving the vicinity to scout out the area.

It had been an eventful day, and nighttime was descending on them rapidly. They were all exhausted now, so after checking up on their yellow eyed friend, they decided to call it a night.

The evening passed by without incident, and the next day Simon organized teams to gather timber, to help build their new campsite. There was no shortage of wood, and as it turned out, a couple of the guys that were there had had experience in construction, so Simon left the task in their capable hands, while he and Elle left the safety of the campsite to scout out the surround areas.

After spending several hours making their way through the forest, they eventually came across the outskirts of a town.

Ahead of them in the clearing was a compound where two canvas backed vehicles were parked up outside a wooden constructed building.

Simon and Elle crawled up to the back of one of the trucks and gently pulled the canvas to one side to peek inside, and were a little shocked at what they found.

Inside the truck were at least a dozen humans bound and gagged and looking quite the worse for wear. Simon checked the other truck, and it was also full of human prisoners.

Elle climbed into the first truck and untied one of the male prisoners, while Simon kept watch.

"Untie the rest of the prisoners while we attempt to start these vehicles to get you out of here," said Elle.

"Thankyou! Who are you?" the prisoner asked Elle.

Elle just said the first thing that came into her head.... "We are the human resistance, and that's our leader Simon. We are here to help you.

As Elle climbed back out of the truck, the door to the wooden building swung open and two huge men walked out and turned in the direction of the trucks. They were obviously the drivers.

Without hesitation Simon and Elle drew their weapons and fired on them slaying them instantly. Elle then ran up to the first guy, and after rifling his pockets she grabbed the keys to the nearest truck and climbed inside.

As Simon went for the keys off the second guy, the door to the building burst open once again, and another two Mycien's emerged and began firing towards Simon's position.

Simon drew his weapon and returned fire, but he was pinned down behind the front wheel of the truck.

Elle then surprised the Myciens, and managed to take one of them out from the safety of the truck window. The final Mycien turned his fire on Elle, and as he did this Simon gambled and ran for the keys to the other truck, but the giant of a man had anticipated his move, and charged towards him.

From out of the blue a gunshot rang out, and the final Mycien crashed to the ground in a splatter of blood. Simon looked up and standing there with weapon in hand, was the prisoner that Elle had freed earlier.

Again, it seemed that Simon was living a charmed life, and had escaped the grip of death thanks to the help of another.

Simon stood up and thanked the prisoner, before climbing into the final truck.

The prisoner returned the thanks for giving him his freedom, but declined to go with them, as he had other business to attend to. He vowed to spread the word about the resistance. Simon and Elle then took off in the direction of the base camp, with several new members of their newly formed resistance on board.

As they pulled up at base camp, Simon disabled the holographic shield long enough for them to pass through the gap in the trees, and they pulled up in the clearing.

There was lots of activity going on, with the felling of trees and people sorting out batches of timber to build various huts around the base. The two construction guys had drawn up some basic design plans, and things were moving on well, and no doubt the additional members of their group, once fed, would definitely help speed up the process.

Inside the trucks, they also found various weapons, from axe's to knives and guns. It seemed that these humans were heading for a gruesome experience if they hadn't been rescued, and they were eternally grateful to Simon and Elle for their freedom.

They also found several maps in the cab of the second truck, showing a full layout of a fifty-mile radius and also various destinations that had been encircled.

"I'm guessing these areas are holding camps, or pit stops for the prisoner runs," said Simon

"Then you know what we must do! We can only defend ourselves in numbers, so the more people we get on our side, the stronger we become" Elle stated.

"Ok... well then I guess we really are the resistance that you claimed us to be" said Simon smiling.

"So, what do you suggest?" asked Elle

"Well, you're the soldier so start training and preparing two teams. I'll head up one group, and you take the other, and let's give these bastards a headache they can't release! Remember no enemy prisoners! And grab as much tech as you can. Straight in and straight out!"

"This is gonna be fun, they won't know what's hit them" said Elle as she hi fived Simon.

It had been a long day for everyone, and it was time to call it a night, and get some well earn rest. Tomorrow the resistance will start to become a reality, and a big thorn in the side of the Myciens.

Simon headed back into the ship and relieved the women looking after the girl in the coma.

Simon sat there looking at her, and just couldn't help wondering who she was? and why she had been separated from the other abductees? She was obviously someone of importance to the merciless Myciens. but until she woke up, then the answers to these questions were just going to elude him. For now, at least, he would just have to wait, and hope she regained consciousness soon.

Simon held her hand and began gently singing old 1950's ballads to her, to try and reach her, and eventually he too drifted off to sleep with her hand still in his....

2

Enforced Captivity

Some months later, Sabrina, a twenty-one-year-old brunette from London, awoke cold, wet, and shivering. She found herself on the floor of a damp, dirty, poorly lit room. Once her eyes had adjusted, she realized that she wasn't alone. A couple of dozen males and females, all aged around twenty to thirty years, were scattered around the edges of the room.

"What the fuck is going on? Who are you people? And where the hell am I?" She screamed angrily.

"Be quiet, you stupid bitch! You're going to get us all killed," came the reply from several voices.

"Hey! There's no need to talk to her like that. Is there?" came a man's voice from the back of the room. "It was a shock the first time for all of us, wasn't it?"

At that moment in time, another girl lying on the floor close to Sabrina also awoke. Only instead of asking questions, she just looked around and started screaming hysterically, much to the annoyance of everyone else in the room. As frightened as Sabrina was, she attempted to comfort her, but the girl was way past reasoning and continued screaming.

A siren sounded, and the room was filled with a flashing red light. Everybody immediately moved to the rear of the room and cowered on the floor.

"Be quiet! Please be quiet" they pleaded to the screaming girl. But to no avail.

Sabrina heard the lock on the door in the front of the room turn, and her eyes widened as she saw a giant of a man followed by a huge dog-like creature. The man issued a command and then released the animal. Snarling and drooling, it ran straight towards the screaming girl and sunk its teeth into her shoulder, spraying Sabrina with her blood. It then proceeded to violently drag her out of the room.

In an instinctual reaction Sabrina reached out to try and help the girl but the giant kicked her to the floor saying ...

"Unless you wanna join your little friend, then I suggest you stay there and shut your mouth."

Shaking with fear she just nodded in agreement, too terrified to talk. Her heart was pounding so fast that she thought her chest was going to explode. she froze with fear, gasping for breath!

"I'll be back to see you lot in a while, until then I don't want any more trouble. So, keep the fucking noise down!" The guard's voice was a deep gravelly bellow.

In Sabrina's terrified state, it registered in her mind that everyone around her in the room had fallen silent and had faced the floor so as not to make eye contact, but Sabrina just couldn't look away. She stared through the doorway in horror and watched the 'dog' tear chunks out of the girl that it had dragged out moments earlier.

The sound of cracking bones and ripping tissue sent shivers through her spine. Tears were streaming down her face, but she remained silent, not wanting to be next on the menu. The man then left closing the door behind him, much to the relief of everyone in the room.

Up to now the guy that had stuck up for Sabrina earlier had been standing at the back of the room with the others, and apart from his little outburst a few moments ago, he'd kept his opinions to himself. But now he felt compelled to help her, so he crawled over to Sabrina who was still sitting on the floor leaning over being physically sick from the shock of what she'd just witnessed.

"It's ok. We'll be ok, we've just got to stay calm" he said trying his best to reassure her. He placed his hand on her shoulder to comfort her.

Unfortunately, this made the situation far worse as the feeling of someone touching her sent Sabrina into a panic.

"Get away from me!" she cried.

"It's Ok! It's Ok. I'm not your enemy; I'm in the same boat as you. Let me help you please" he pleaded.

"How the hell can you help me?" she yelled at him.

"Hey, fuck her!" said a male voice from the back of the room. "She can wallow in her own self-pity for all I care. Stupid bitch!"

"Hey, fuck you mate. That's a bit harsh, isn't it? Luckily, we're not all heartless bastards like you eh"

"Who the hell do you think you're talking to, you little prick?" said the guy at the back.

In response to this the lad that was talking to Sabrina jumped up and unleashed several punches on the advancing guy and knocked him to the floor. Before he had a chance to recover, he then pinned him to the ground and reigned punches down on his face rendering him unconscious.

He then stood up and turned to the rest of the group in the room. "Anyone have anything else to say? Come on get it off your chest! Well?... Just as I thought. Right! My name's Chris and this is how it's going to be. From now on we are going to fucking help each other. We're much stronger together than we are apart. We can start by exchanging stories and then maybe, just maybe we'll figure out what the fucks going on here!" Chris went on to say, "Second, this girl over here needs our help and support, so please ladies ... go and fucking help her. Let's get on with it then; we may not have much time!"

His speech seemed to lift the group, giving them something else to focus on. They say that amidst chaos there's always order in leadership, and it seemed that Chris had just assumed that roll.

Chris looked around and caught Sabrina's eye as she glanced up at him, and just nodded towards him as if to thank him for sticking up for her.

Over the next hour or so the group began to introduce themselves to each other and exchanged stories of alien abductions. It now seemed obvious to everyone that they all had many things in common: their age group, the fact that they were all taken alone with little or no witnesses, and that they all remembered the circumstances of their abductions and then nothing until waking up here.

Chris had been the first of the group to awaken from his ordeal and over the next couple of days the rest of the group had also come around. He had witnessed several attacks from the dog-like creature, as had several others in the room, and it was every bit as horrifying each time. There was a trough of water in the corner and what could only be described as a bucket of what looked like liquidized food that had been topped up twice since they had been conscious.

Whilst Chris was chatting to another guy in the room, he felt a hand touch his shoulder and he turned around to see Sabrina standing there.

"Hi ... Sorry about earlier, I couldn't ..."

"It's ok. I reacted the same way the first time I saw that happen. It was sickening and horrifying to watch, not to mention being confused and disorientated from the circumstances we now find ourselves in"

Sabrina burst into tears again.

It was clear to Chris as he looked deep into her eyes, that Sabrina was obviously still traumatized and probably felt a little guilty at not being able to prevent the death of the unfortunate girl.

"Hey ... There was nothing that you have done to save her. In fact, you had far more courage than the rest of us. That was very brave of you to try and help her"

"No, it was very stupid of me to do that. Thanks for sticking up for me with that guy, though"

"I don't think he'll be giving anyone else any more trouble... It's me who should be thanking you... You gave me the strength and excuse to speak up which seems to have made everyone stronger"

"Thanks anyway. My name's Sabrina" she said giving him a hug.

The two of them then sat down on the cold hard floor and chatted for a while. Sabrina told Chris that she'd been out walking her dog when she'd seen a bright light appear above her. The next thing she remembered was waking up here.

Chris had a similar tale and was taken whilst on his way home from a night out on the town. "To be honest with you, I was far too drunk to remember anything. One minute I was outside a club in Essex and the next thing I remember I was here" he told her.

After about an hour or so the sound of footsteps approaching the door was heard once again.

"Ok ... Everyone to the back of the room and keep quiet," said Chris. "Don't give them any reason to hurt us."

The door swung open and once again the large figure of the man re-entered the room, this time accompanied by two others of similar build.

"Right listen carefully. I won't be repeating myself. You will now make up two lines, males to the left and females to the right. You will then be escorted to our sanitation department where you will be cleaned and disinfected. From there you will be taken to a holding camp where you will then await further instructions."

"What's going on? Why are we here?" Chris asked tentatively.

One of the three guards for want of a better word approached and prodded him with what looked like a six-inch metal rod. As soon as it contacted him, a blue spark sent a shock wave throughout his body, causing him to fall to the ground writhing in agony. The sounds of gasps could be heard throughout the room.

"Take that as a warning to you all" he shouted. "Do not interrupt me again. You do not speak unless your asked to! The next person to do that will be severely punished. Do you understand?" he barked out at the group.

This time everybody just nodded and bowed their heads in respect for fear of reprisal.

"Well ... What are you waiting for? Lineup!"

Without any further a due or argument, the group followed their instructions. Still feeling stunned from the guard's attack, Chris slowly climbed to his feet and was surprised to see the outstretched hand of the guy that he'd had the fight with earlier.

"Let me help you, it's my way of saying sorry for acting like a dickhead before. It's the least I can do."

"It's not me you should be apologizing to."

"I know, and I will apologize to her too. Look I'm not usually like that. I was just scared that's all."

"You're not the only one in a fucked-up place you know, you've just got to deal with it, mate. We're all in this together."

"You're right of course. Please accept my apology. ... I'm George from Bulgaria."

George grabbed his arm and helped him to his feet. The three guards then escorted them out of the room and down a long corridor towards a brightly lit entranceway which opened out into a huge sun lit courtyard. As they looked around it became apparent that they weren't suffering alone. There must have been several hundred people all standing in lines looking disheveled and dirty from their ordeal. Many were crying and most of them looked frightened. The sound of whispering voices and sobbing people, both men and women, was a heart wrenching sight indeed, enough to send terror into the bravest of souls.

"Oh my god, this looks really bad!" said George

"You don't say! And look up there, what the hell is that?" Chris said pointing to the sky.

"Oh fuck!.. There are two suns. How is that possible?"

"Well, I guess we're not in Kansas anymore ... Like you said, this doesn't look good at all!"

Sabrina who had also noticed the double sun just looked up in horror. It was clear to everyone that they were in big trouble now.

Once all the people had been gathered up, they were told to follow the path out of the compound and on through a forested area. They were of course escorted by many guards, several of which had dogs which were constantly snapping at their heels to drive them forward. The guards indiscriminately gave mild shocks to anyone they felt was lagging behind, and several people suffered the ultimate fate as they just couldn't keep up. They were merely executed, and their bodies were left where they fell.

Eventually they reached a large concrete structure and were led inside a huge holding room which had been divided into two by a large glass screen. Males were put on one side and females were funneled into the other. Once they were inside, they were instructed to discard all clothes and possessions and they were led one by one through a doorway at the end of the room.

"Oh my god! This is all too familiar" Chris said sounding extremely concerned.

"What do you mean by that?" asked George.

"I'm talking about the holocaust in the second world war. I hope to God that that isn't what's about to happen here."

On over hearing this, several of the guys standing next to Chris and George panicked and ran towards the entranceway as if to escape. It was a futile effort, as the doors were heavily guarded by these eight-foot-tall men. The first of the three escapees was instantly grabbed by the throat and lifted off the floor with ease, before having his neck snapped. The other two attempted to fight their way past the guards, but their punches had little or no effect, and they were quickly subdued and consequently killed.

"Get back in line now" Screamed the guards.

Suffice to say the people instantly complied, and without further delay they we're quickly funnelled through the doors at the end of the room, where they were hosed down and scrubbed with chemicals. After this they emerged through yet another door into a large open courtyard where they were given a grey crudely made uniform, and then moved into two huge holding cages that separated the males from the females.

"Attention ... Attention" came the sound over the loudspeaker system.

"You are now on the planet Teemor, and you are the property of the of the Mycien guard. If you comply with our requests without trouble, then you will not be harmed. Should you decide to resist, then have no doubt in your minds, you will be executed. Tomorrow you will be moved to a new location where you will be assigned to your destination."

The sound system then fell silent and after the cages were locked, most of the Mycien guards left the compound and were replaced by human guards that were carrying the shock sticks that Chris and several other people had had the misfortune of experiencing earlier. The sight of this angered many people and as a result, insults were traded between them and the human guards.

The hours passed by slowly, and eventually darkness fell upon the courtyard. George and Chris, both found it impossible to sleep over the sound of men and women crying. They just sat by the bars of the cage watching the guards and discussing ways of escaping. As they were doing this, one of the guards walking past overheard their conversation.

"I'd forget that if I were you," he said pointing his stick towards them.

"How the fuck can you live with yourself, imprisoning your own kind?"

"Hey, I'd rather be out here than in there with you, mate." Said the guard. "I've been there, done that and I don't want to do it again. Besides, there's little I can do to help you. You just wanna hope you get the right destination tomorrow."

The human guard was dressed in a smart blue uniform, and it was clear to Chris by his healthy look and attire that he was being well fed and well looked after for the job that he was doing. Chris knew that the chances of him helping them was slim to none, but he had to ask anyway.

"Can't you help us at all?" asked Chris.

"I'm sorry, but we're under surveillance here, so I can't help you. All I can tell you is that you're on one of three trading planets, and tomorrow you will be sent to a colony auction where your fate will be decided."

"Why have they separated the men from the women?"

"Because the women will mainly be impregnated to host the off-spring of certain races as they cannot conceive children of their own anymore. They don't want them falling pregnant before this process, otherwise there only use would be as servants or the games"

"What do you mean by the games?" asked Chris.

"That's enough, I've said too much already. Now keep it down, and don't give me reason to hurt you"

"But ..."

"Enough!" he said sparking his stick against the bars.

Through the night several people were stunned by the guards for hurling abuse at them, but eventually the morning came around, and the Mycien guards returned to release the people before leading them onto some waiting vehicles, which drove them several miles away into a busy city center.

The busses parked up, and everyone was corralled into a large open area, where they were set down in their groups. Looking around, you could see streets going off in all directions, and in the center of the square was a stage like structure with steps either side of it.

The ground that they were standing on was very gravelly, and the buildings that surrounded the square were very low tech indeed. Most of them seemed to be made of wood, which was pretty strange considering that they'd been brought here by a very high-tech craft. A wooden railing separated the prisoners from a gathering crowd, and there seemed to be quite a bit of activity around the stage area.

"Well, what do you think?" George inquired.

"I think this is the auction and we are the merchandise," Chris replied.

"We could try and make a break for it."

"George, there are guards posted at the entrances to each of the streets, and in case you hadn't noticed, they're not just carrying shock sticks. Those look a lot like guns around their waists, not to mention the fact that they are much more powerful than us"

"Hey, I thought you had more balls than that. You were a big man back in the room. What happened?"

"Look, I didn't say I wouldn't try, but we have to pick our moment, or well get slaughtered before we have a chance to get away"

Chris looked up towards the girls and caught sight of Sabrina who was discreetly waving at him. He signaled back at her to ask if she was OK, and she nodded towards him. Shortly after this, several vehicles arrived carrying an entourage of strange looking people that were definitely not from Earth.

"It looks like the buyers have arrived," said George

There were several different groups of unsavory looking characters. The Mycien guards began parading the women one by one across the stage, where they were inspected like cattle and then bid upon by the buyers, some of whom were particularly brutal with their newly acquired humans. One particular girl, through panic or fear, tried to resist by striking out at her new owner. She was instantly grabbed by her hair and lifted into the air, still screaming. Her body was then slammed down onto the handrail in front of the onlooking crowd, snapping her back like a twig and instantly silencing her screams.

The human prisoners gasped as they witnessed what had just occurred, and panic set in amongst them. In the pandemonium that followed, people began running towards the streets that surrounded the square. The guards instantly reacted by drawing their weapons and indiscriminately firing on the humans with beams of light, that seriously maimed or simply killed whoever they encountered.

"Now's our chance!" said George. "If we're going to do it, it has to be now!"

"Wait ... I must save Sabrina," Chris said beckoning over to her. Sabrina didn't need to be asked twice. She ran towards him and once she'd reached him, he grabbed her hand.

"Ok let's do it, let's go!" Chris shouted as they ran towards one of the exits.

The three of them joined another large group that were also heading in the same direction. By the time they reached the junction, the uprising behind them was quickly being quelled, and the guards were beginning to round up and retake control of the prisoners. The escaping group that they were part of, had been whittled down to about a dozen, as several had been picked off along the way.

There was only one Mycien and several human guards protecting the exit to the square, so they decided to run the gauntlet as they were now in a do-or-die situation. The human guards were soon over run as the group scampered past them. But as Chris tried to pass, the Mycien guard grabbed him by the throat and lifted him off the ground. This seemed to be a favorite killing technique for the Myciens. Just as Chris felt his neck about to snap, a flash of light penetrated the guards head, sending pieces of his flesh spraying out in the air. The guard then released his grip and collapsed to the floor, dead.

"Come on! Get up, you've got to go now!" a voice screamed at Chris.

He scrambled to his feet with the help of the guy that had just shot the guard and fled down the street with his newfound friend and of course, amongst others, George and Sabrina.

"This way. Follow us if you want to live" said the Mycien assassin as he led them down a muddy side street.

"Now quickly, everybody come close to me and put you backs against this wall here" He pointed to the spot where he wanted them. The assassin hoarded everyone into place and told them to stand dead still. He then activated a device strapped to his wrist.

"Whatever you do, do not move a muscle!" he said.

Moments later, several of the Mycien guards turned the corner and ran in their direction. Again, he told them to stay still and not to make a sound.

Sabrina tightly squeezed Chris's hand, and he could feel her shaking and her pulse racing as the guards closed in on their position. But to their surprise they ran straight past them, as if they weren't there.

"What happened? How come they didn't see us?" whispered Sabrina.

"I activated a holographic shield; it copies the background and masks our vital signs. Breathing, scent, body heat. It makes us virtually invisible to the onlooking eye. Cool or what, eh!" said the assassin smiling. "There are many devices like this if you have the cash to buy them. These devices help us to level the playing field"

"Who's us? Sabrina asked him.

"I'm Simon, and I lead the resistance. This race selected the wrong colony of humans to fuck with," he said, smiling. He seemed to be enjoying himself!

"The wrong what ...?" both Sabrina and Chris asked at the same time.

"Look, I'll be happy to answer all your questions, but right now we must move to a safe location. We can only fool them for so long, so we need to get to safety right now, OK."

3

Joining The Resistance

After an hour or so of scurrying down muddy alleyways, they were eventually led into an obscure and run-down building at the far edge of town.

"Thank God for that! I don't think I could have taken another step; my feet are killing me, and my legs are so sore," said Sabrina.

"Yes, I'm feeling the same" replied Chris, still panting for breath.

Simon led them into a large room that was sparsely furnished, drab in color and only lit by the flickering flames in the large fireplace in the center of the room. As they sat down on the floor in front of the fire, Chris couldn't help but notice the many footprints imprinted in the layer of dust that covered the floor. It was obvious to him that they weren't the first group of people that had passed this way.

"Sabrina, come and sit by the fire. You're shivering with cold."

"Thanks, I think I will" She replied. As she sat down, Chris took off his jacket and placed it around her shoulders. He'd had a Christian upbringing, and although his family were not heavily religious, they had managed to instill him with Christian values and taught him to respect others and to always be chivalrous and polite to those in need.

"See, I told you everything would be alright," he said hugging her.

"Yes, you did, but you didn't say anything about running for our lives and having sore feet," she said, smiling.

"No maybe not, but we're still alive, aren't we, which proves if nothing else that you should always be positive in life. I have a tattoo on my chest which simply reads, 'never give up never surrender.' it's all about karma, Sabrina. Positivity breeds positivity"

"I like you Chris, there's something about you that makes me feel like I've known you for years. I feel like I could tell you anything. You have a great outlook on life."

Over the next hour or so several other small groups of escapees began arriving, swelling the numbers to around 40 confused people. He continued to grow closer to Sabrina, and he eventually plucked up the courage to put his arm around her and pulled her in close to keep her warm.

Several minutes later the door to the room swung open and Simon walked in and addressed the room. "Ok ...! Listen up everyone. Quiet, please, settle down... Now I know your all scared, and you've been through a terrible ordeal already, so I'm going to fill you in on the basics of what's going on here. In case you hadn't worked it out yet, you're not on Earth anymore! You are in fact on the planet Teemor in the Garda quadrant. One way or another you were all abducted and brought here by a barbaric colony of humans called the Myciens, to be sold and used as currency.

"Why ... Why would they do that?" came the response from the room.

Simon went on to explain, "For want of a better word, they are mercenaries and slave traders with ideas above their station. They send out snatch squads to capture what they call merchandise. They then sell the merchandise so that they can advance themselves by buying technology from the other more advanced human colonies."

"That's the second time you've mentioned 'human colonies,"
Chris said. "How can these Myciens be human? Their physiology is totally different to ours, and how many colonies are there

anyway?"

"I can assure you they are of human origin. In fact, there are nine colonies, all of which have differences in abilities and physiology. Or at least there were nine colonies, the 8th colony was practically wiped out in a war with the Myciens. They found out that they were kidnaping their people and decided to fight back. Unfortunately, they lost due to the advanced technology they were fighting against. The destruction of the 8th colony forced the Myciens to look elsewhere for merchandise to acquire, and they discovered Earth, the 9th and final colony of humanity.

"So, you're telling us," Chris said, "that our origins are not from the big bang theory of evolution, but that we are one of a various set of colonies placed on Earth thousands of years ago to advance humanity? No way!"

"Look I know it's a lot to take in, but it is how it is!" said Simon. "The Myciens have no reasoning abilities; they are driven purely by greed and ambition. They have little or no conscience, which makes them extremely dangerous. This is where we come in. We have formed a resistance group, and our numbers are growing. Now you're welcome to take your chances on your own, or you can join us, it's up to you."

At this point one of Simon's henchmen stepped in and asked everyone in the room to keep quiet and to let Simon finish his address before asking anymore questions.

"It's OK, I'll answer their questions," said Simon.

"What do you mean 'join you`? Do you mean fight them?"

"Yes, I mean fight. Look, the fact of the matter is that you're on another planet being hunted down by a ruthless race of people that have no respect for your colony whatsoever. So, you have two options: You run and hide, or you stand with us and fight. It's your choice"

"But what chance would we have? The last race that tried that we're all but wiped out, and that was a whole planet!"

"True but they were up against superior weaponry," said Simon.

"I hate to burst your bubble, mate, but aside of the overwhelming numbers that we're up against, so are we!"

"Yes, but the difference is, we are on their planet. We have access to the same weapons and technology as they do, and through organized, targeted attacks we can affect them and hopefully draw attention of our plight to some of the other, more sympathetic colonies"

Soon after this Simon left the room, leaving everyone to ponder on their decision.

Chris held tightly onto Sabrina's hand as he rolled around everything in his head that Simon had just told them. There certainly was a lot to take in.

His concentration was eventually broken by Sabrina as she whispered in his ear. "Well? What do you think?"

"I don't think we have a choice. I for one certainly don't fancy our chances without them."

"No, I think you're right. We should join them; it's our best chance," She replied, giving Chris a hug.

As she pulled back from him, she caressed the bruises on his neck, "Does that hurt?" she asked looking concerned.

"Well funny enough it does a little," he replied laughing.

"That's the first time I've seen you laugh. You have a great smile," said Sabrina.

"Thanks. So, do you." Chris said, leaning over to kiss her.

As soon as their lips touched, the door of the room opened again. Simon came in rolling a trolly full of hot food and water and told them to eat up. He went on to say that this was one of several safe houses that they had, but they couldn't stay here too long as recently the Myciens had started conducting house-to-house searches. At first, they hadn't done this, but as the resistance numbers had grown and the attacks became more frequent, they were now at the stage where they had no choice but to sit up and take notice. Simon also told them that only 25 per cent of this planet was inhabitable, and many of them were off-planet doing what they did, so the odds weren't as bad as they seemed.

Chris spoke up. "So, if, as you say, they treat us with such contempt, then how do you manage to acquire properties to use as safe houses without getting caught?"

"As I said earlier, there are now eight colonies in total, and amongst them there are many sympathizers for our plight. On each of the eight planets there are residents residing from all the races. Not everybody agrees with the Myciens philosophy; in fact many of them feel that it's nothing short of criminal and barbaric, and the destruction of the eighth colony was practically genocide."

"So, what you're saying then is that you have powerful allies?"

"Yes... we'll, Sort of. We do have allies, but right now they are in the minority. We're hoping that if we can cause enough commotion, then others will sit up and take notice! That's the plan anyway," he replied with a smile.

"Well, we don't need to think about it anymore, do we Sabrina?"

"No, we don't. We are both happy to join you"

"That's great news," said Simon. He shook Chris's hand and gave Sabrina a hug.

Chris wasn't the only one to take this choice, as most of the others in the room had also decided to join Simon's band of merry men. Still, a handful of people had decided to take their chances on their own. There were no hard feelings, and Simon was happy to give them ample supplies of food and water to take with them. The remaining people were divided into a few different groups. Two groups were taken to a different location, leaving a dozen or so in the safe house with Simon.

"What will happen to the few people who took their chances on their own?" Asked Chris.

The look on Simon's face said it all; it was obvious that their chance's were slim at best.

"Ok, you can all bed down here for the night. Try and get some sleep, tomorrow well start your training. Good night" He threw down some bed linen before leaving the room.

"I guess tomorrow we're going to become soldiers," said Sabrina cuddling up next to Chris in front of the fire.

"Yes, I suppose so. Funny how things work out, isn't it. Last week I was a computer programmer, and this week I'm a soldier for the resistance in another universe. Crazy or what, you just couldn't write this stuff."

"I know what you mean. Last week I was a nurse and this week a soldier of fortune" said Sabrina laughing.

"Oh, so you're used to dealing with blood and guts then" Chris said sarcastically.

"Not like this! I've never felt so traumatized and helpless in all my life as when I saw that girl get ripped apart. That was terrible."

"Yeah, I know. It was shocking, and I'm betting we're going to see a lot more of that before too long. It's a little scary, isn't it"

"Yeah. I think we should get some sleep. Goodnight" she kissed Chris on the cheek before cuddling up to him.

Chris lay there next to Sabrina thinking that this wasn't such a bad deal after all. A new start to his hum drum life, albeit a little frightening and without doubt fraught with danger, but he seemed to have found a new and attractive companion in Sabrina. He'd have to say that she was his type. Brunette, long hair, and fair in completion. No, not so bad after all, he thought as he drifted off to sleep in her arms.

The next morning, they were awoken to the aroma of hot tea, or at least it looked and smelled like hot tea.

"Oh my god! What the fuck is that it tastes awful" Chris blurted out after taking a sip.

"It's best if you don't ask," said Simon laughing "don't spit it out, just drink it. It's full of nutrients"

The fire had burnt down to nothing overnight, and there was a distinct chill in the air. With that in mind, they decided to drink the nasty beverage, as did the others in the room.

George seemed to have made a friend amongst Simon's resistance fighters. Like most of the others she was in her late twenties. She had shoulder-length auburn hair. Chris looked over at her and could see that she had beautiful blue eyes and a European sort of look to her face, although by her accent he could tell that she was definitely English. She was approximately five feet six tall and slim but muscularly defined. George introduced her as Elle.

"Hi, Elle, pleased to meet you. I'm Chris and this is Sabrina. So ... How are you bearing up?"

"Fine actually," she said aggressively. "In fact, I'm raring to go and ready to kick some Mycien arse!"

"Not a shy girl then" Chris said jokingly to George.

Elle went on to explain that she was abducted and imprisoned on the same craft as Simon whilst on leave from the army and had served on several battlefronts in her time.

"A regular GI Jane then," said Sabrina, laughing. "I'm sticking close behind you."

"Yeah, me too" said Chris giggling with her.

Elle seemed ok; she had her head screwed on right. If anything, Chris sort of felt the odd one out. He had learned in talking with George that he'd spent two years in the Bulgarian army, albeit conscripted, and of course there was his new girlfriend GI Jane here. Even Sabrina was helpful, as she was a trained nurse, but how did he fit in? He was just a simple computer tech; what could he possibly do to help? The only thing that he might be able to bring to the table was the fact that he had run and managed large teams of people in the work that he'd done. He wasn't afraid of taking chances or making the right decisions difficult or otherwise. Hopefully this would stand him in good stead in the future.

The tea was followed by a bite to eat, and they were then taken down into the basement where they began practicing self-defense and of course taught how to use their weapons. George was a natural of course; Sabrina and Chris took a little longer to adjust.

During the time they spent trying to master their devices, they all got to know each other much better, and Chris now also seemed to be getting on with George despite their disastrous opening introduction. He was a nice guy, and best of all he wasn't false in anyway; what you saw is what you got with George. Chris for one, respected that in a person. Even at this early stage it was obvious that they were all going to get on famously.

It was late afternoon now and it had been a long and tiring day. Simon called time on the training, and they all went back upstairs for some nourishment. After they'd finished eating, Simon told them that he had been reliably informed that one of the buyers from the auction was moving out and was heading for the landing pad where his ship was moored five sectors from here. Accompanying him would be several guards and a bus load of his newly acquired concubines, not to mention whatever technology they might have with them.

"Ok, first of all, what do you mean 'concubines?" asked Chris.

"How far is five sectors, and what are we going to do if we find them?"

"What do you think we're going to do? Obviously, we're going to rescue the concubines, defeat the guards, and take what we can to help the cause.

Simon went on to explain what it means to be a concubine. The buyers are rich influential people that come from the various colonies. They buy colonists from the Myciens as slaves, and thereby perpetuate the problem. The main reason they buy the girls is to impregnate them. They are taken back, stripped naked, and sexually assaulted over and over until they become pregnant. On top of this the human girls cannot carry their children full term as it would kill both the child and the girl because of the differences in physiology. After six months, the girls are strapped down, and the child is cut out of them while there still awake. No anesthetics are used for fear of damaging the child and like the girl on stage, the bodies of the girls are then discarded like garbage"

"I don't understand why they use captured humans instead of their own women," said Chris.

"There is a big problem with infertility amongst certain colonies due to a highly contagious virus that swept through the planets a decade ago.

Chris felt shocked and sickened at what Simon was telling him. How could these people be so heartless? It was difficult to take it all in, and he didn't want to hear anymore, but his curiosity would eat away at him if he didn't listen to all that Simon had to tell him.

"Well, I guess that explains supply and demand," he said, "but what if they find the human girls to be infertile? what happens then?"

"Then they are passed on as servants or for entertainment at the Gozian games"

"Dare I ask!"

"Please do. It's important that you all understand everything that's going on here!" said Simon.

"So, tell us ... What happens at the games?" Chris asked him.

"I suppose the easiest way to explain it would be to compare it to the colosseum in Rome. Basically, they are slaughtered for the sake of a paying public. Trust me, it's not a pretty sight; if they're lucky, they die quickly.

"You said that some of the colonists were sympathetic to your cause. Can't they help us?"

"Yes, they are and they can, but as I said, their numbers are small, and they are not prepared to openly go into bat for us... not just yet anyway. Oh, and in answer to your other question, five sectors are about fifty miles away. The buyer and his entourage will probably be heavily armed, so we all need to stay alert"

Chris turned his gaze to Sabrina, who had been standing by his side listening intently to what was being said and was now squeezing Chris's hand very tightly to grab his attention. She wanted to ask questions of her own.

"So why do they put such little value on our lives?" she asked

"Some would say that it's because we are so far behind them in technological advancement, others feel that they are just a far superior race and that we are no more than pets or merchandise to them. But as I said, not everyone feels that way. Which is why we must cause them as many problems as we can."

"Seems to me that if you want to make them sit up and take notice," said Sabrina, "then you should be causing problems in the other colonies' home worlds as well. Like you said earlier, the Myciens are just mercenaries who have no respect for us. Our best chance would be to disrupt the colonies that might be persuaded to help us"

"Hmm, you might have a point there." Said Simon "But for the moment at least, we have an opportunity to stop this buyer from enslaving more humans, and maybe pick up some tech on the way."

"So, when do we leave?" asked Chris.

"There's no time like the present, so I need everyone to be ready to go in about ten minutes time,"

He then asked them to wait by the door and said that as soon as he gave the signal, they were to head outside and follow the instructions given to them.

Before they knew it, the call came, and they were led outside to several waiting canvas backed vehicles which quickly disembarked and headed off in the direction of the target. There was quite a buzz around now, although like Sabrina, Chris was very scared and concerned at what was to come. George and Elle on the other hand were up for it, but then they had been in this situation before, what with their military backgrounds.

It took just over an hour to catch up with the buyer's convoy, which consisted of several vehicles. Chris could clearly see them in the distance through the trail of dust that they were leaving behind. The ground that they were driving on was very desert like and barren, with mountain ranges to either side. It reminded him of the old western films that he used to watch as a child.

As they moved forward, they came to a fork in the road, and it was clear that they had taken the path directly ahead. So, Simon gave the order to take the path on the right as he explained to Chris that apparently this was a short cut that would get them ahead of the convoy that they were following. Sure, enough he was correct. Simon headed uphill and passed them from above without them even realizing that he was there. He drove back down the hill and rejoined the track several minutes ahead of them.

"Right, everybody out!" came the shout from Simon as the trucks ground to a halt.

4

The Calm before the Storm

They climbed from their vehicles and headed for the trees. One of Simon's men propped up the bonnet before joining them. The other two trucks were pulled around the corner out of sight and they laid there in wait for the event to begin. They didn't have to wait too long before the oncoming convoy arrived, stopping about twenty yards behind the apparently broken-down vehicle.

Several characters stepped out and slowly approached the truck, calling out to try and get a response. When they didn't receive one, they immediately drew their weapons and moved in fast to surround the vehicle.

"Not yet ... stay down and hold your fire" was the command quickly passed among Simon's men.

As they crouched down in the brush it became apparent to the recent recruits that talking about what they were going to do earlier, although very inspiring at the time, was in reality an extremely frightening experience, especially as several of them had never even held a gun let alone shot someone with one!

It wasn't long before the security detail realized the truck was abandoned and began to push it off the road. The next thing that happened was a massive explosion as Simon remotely detonated the truck, killing the guards instantly.

"Now! Let's go!" screamed Simon as he rose from the brush and headed towards the convoy of vehicles.

Instinctually everyone else stood up and blindly followed him. With ash and debris still falling from the initial blast. A gun battle ensued, with the guards killing several of the resistance fighters as they advanced towards them. Luckily though, they still outnumbered the guards and soon overran them. But as they celebrated their victory, the rear truck in the convoy, which was holding some of the human slaves, exploded, silencing the cheers and knocking several people to the ground from the blast.

As Chris climbed to his feet, he could see Simon through the smoke dragging someone out of the middle vehicle and throwing him to the ground, which was now strew with vehicle and body parts. The blast had killed a handful of the prisoners on the rear truck, and as Chris approached the small figure of a man at Simon's feet, it became apparent to him from the device still in his hand, that he was the one responsible for this atrocity. This five-foot-tall fat little man who was obviously someone of note judging by the clothes and jewelry that adorned him, was now reduced to scrambling about in the dirt, screaming out obscenities in a strange language.

"What's he saying?" Chris asked.

"Let's find out, shall we?" Simon replied.

Two of the resistance fighters held him down while Simon attached a collar around his neck and activated it. Instantly as if by magic he began speaking the King's English, albeit with an electronical tone.

"Release me now! I command you! You are nothing but vermin, and you will pay for this outrage" he screamed.

"You are not in any position to tell us what to do, fat boy" snarled Simon.

"Do you know who I am? I will have you hunted down and tortured for what you have done here today. You will die a painful death for your crimes."

"You are the vermin here, and believe me when I say this: We will continue to hunt your kind down to eradicate scum like you, until your race and others like you change your attitude towards us. This is the message that you will be taking back with you dead or alive you piece of shit."

Simon told his men to hold his head tightly as he pulled out a knife and carved the letters HR on his forehead, ignoring the screams and obvious agony that this caused him. He then stepped back and turned to walk away.

The buyer immediately stopped yelling, looked up at Simon, and screamed out the words: "Kill him! kill him now!"

The two resistance men that were holding the buyer instantly released him, drew their weapons and fired on Simon. There was a flash of light and a thudding sound as the shots impacted the back of his body, knocking him to the ground. Elle then instantly stepped forward and shot the buyer in the head. As his blood-stained body hit the dirt, Simon's two assassins also crumpled to the ground fully unconscious. Everything had happened so quickly.

Once the commotion had settled down, all eyes turned towards Simon their leader, who was now gingerly climbing to his feet.

"No way! George blurted out.

"How the hell is that possible? We all saw you get shot ... You should be dead!"

"Remember what I said to you about devices" he said, smiling whilst trying to catch his breath.

"Of course, Why do you ask?" George responded. Simon opened his jacket to reveal yet another gadget that was strapped to his chest.

"Like I said, it's all about evening the odds. This is a personal force field; it can be set to different frequencies to protect you from the blast of certain weapons. In this case our own!"

"Clever bastard ... You knew that was going to happen, didn't you? But how could you be so sure that your own men would turn against you?"

"The buyer that we were holding, was a Gozian. His race is capable of many mind tricks as you saw with my men. They can target the minds of most of the different races. When Elle shot him, the hold he had on my men was instantly released, as you saw."

"So... Elle knew this as well?" George asked him.

"Yes of course, I filled her in on my plan last night. I wanted to demonstrate his ability's and show everyone what the Gozians are capable of"

"You're fucking crazy. That could easily have gone wrong! And if that's supposed to be a force field, then how come it knocked you to the ground?"

"The shield minimalizes the weapons effects, but at that range you will still feel the kinetic impact of the blast."

"So why hasn't everyone got one of these devices?"

"Because we only have so many of them right now. This is something we're trying to address. Besides they're only effective on light weapons, if you have the correct frequency"

Simon then walked over to Elle and thanked her for her part in the demonstration. There was a feeling now of jubilation and belief in the cause amongst everyone, and shots were fired in the air in celebration of their victory. The remaining trucks were then requisitioned, and the Gozian and his now deceased guards were stripped of all weapons and devices. The remaining captives were then released from their shackles and secured into the canvas-backed vehicles that they'd arrived in.

"Ok, gather your shit it's time to go," shouted Simon

Once everyone had climbed into the backs of the trucks, they left the carnage behind them and headed off in an easterly direction.

"Are we heading for the landing pad now?" George asked the driver.

"No chance. We're getting the hell out of here before they realize he's missing."

"What happens then?"

"They'll send out a search party for him, and once they find his body, they'll come looking for us, and it won't be with trucks and small arms fire. We wouldn't stand a chance against them."

"So why did Simon carve the letters HR in his forehead?"

"It stands for human resistance of course. Simon was a bit of a film buff on earth. He said he'd seen it once in a movie.

It's to let them know that we won't tolerate their shit any longer, although I've got to admit that it's a step up on what we've done up to now"

"How do you mean?"

"I mean that we've never attacked and killed a Gozian convoy before. They are one of the most feared and powerful races out there, and they won't take this lying down," said the driver, sounding quite worried.

The trucks drove for about an hour before pulling to a halt in a densely forested area. Simon said, "Ok, everybody out and follow me please"

"Follow you where?" said Chris, looking a little puzzled. We're surrounded by woodland and the trail ends here"

"Watch and learn, my friend, watch and learn" replied Simon smiling to himself. He then tapped the device on his wrist and an opening appeared to his right, lighting up the Forrest in front of it.

"So ... Where does this lead to then?" asked Sabrina

"Base camp of course!" replied Simon.

Simon led everyone through the doorway and into a large clearing in the forest that had been artificially lit with portable lights. Various temporary structures surrounded a large empty space, and there were lots of people milling around, looking preoccupied with whatever it was that they were doing.

"Wow! How's this possible?" asked Chris.

"It's similar to the force shield I used when we were running from the auction, only this one's more powerful"

"No shit, Sherlock."

"That was a portable force shield. This one is powered by our first and finest acquisition yet. It covers a much larger area and like the portable shield it simply mimics its surroundings and makes us invisible to onlooking eyes. The difference is its stable, so we can move around inside it without being detected"

"So, what's powering it? And what's this finest acquisition that you have?"

"It's right in front of you. Behold!" replied Simon as he pressed yet another button on his magical wrist device.

Suddenly a large black disc the size of a small house materialized, filling up the empty space that was previously in front of them. Chris, Sabrina, and the others gasped in amazement.

"It's a ship. Wow, this is incredible!"

"Yes, it's a ship. It's what brought me here. It's one of many that the Myciens have... or, I should say, had."

"How the hell did you manage to acquire this?"

Simon explained that while he was being transported in the slave ship that was now visibly in front of them, the device that was keeping him and many other captives alive and unconscious had malfunctioned as it entered the Garda quadrant. Everyone including the crew were still in some sort of cryosleep. Elle's cryo tube opened first, and once she was conscious, she had revived him and the dozen or so other prisoners that were on board, not including the crew. Elle was running a bit of a fever and looked extremely unwell, so Simon told her to take it easy while he proceeded to check out the crews cryo tubes. He didn't want to take any chances, so they eliminated all of them barring one. You know what they say, it's better to be safe than sorry.

The next problem that he had was that they couldn't understand the instrument panels, as they were written in a strange language.

The only other option left to him, was to take a chance and wake up the final crew member.

They bound and revived him to try and get some answers and were surprised to find that he not only understood them, but after a while, he also spoke perfect English.

"Really." Chris was smiling in disbelief. "I feel like I'm going to wake up in a minute from some sort of weird sci-fi dream."

"I can assure you that this is no dream, and it's as real as you and me, I'm afraid"

"So, what happened next?"

Simon went on to explain that their problems had started once they'd revived the guard. After his life was threatened, the guard agreed to land the craft, but unbeknown to them, he'd managed to lock up the controls and set us on a course to this planet. Once he'd done that, he took great pleasure in letting them know what he'd done.

It was clear to Simon that they were now heading into a trap and there was very little that he could do about it. In the moments that followed, the Mycien broke free and attacked the two guys that were watching him and then turned to run towards him with murder in his eyes. At that moment Simon believed his life would end, but to his surprise and relief Elle appeared and shot him several times in the head and chest. Simon then took the weapon from Elle and fired at the navigation panel which knocked them off course and they crash-landed here in the Forrest.

"Well, it's obvious you've managed to work out their devices then. So, my question must be, why don't you just leave? Why stay and fight? "

"Your right, we have worked out their technology in general," said Simon, "but we can't fly the thing. Its password protected and we can't override it!"

"Well, you may have just struck gold then."

"How do you mean?"

"I'm a computer programmer. I write software for different companies ... Well, I used to anyway. I could have a look at it, if you like, although someone will have to help me translate the commands as I go."

"That won't be necessary," said Simon. "Tilt your head to one side for me,"

Chris did as he was asked, and Simon then pulled out a small device that looked a bit like a diabetic's pen. He pressed it against Chris's neck and clicked the button on the end.

"Ouch! What the hell was that for?"

"It's a universal translator. Now you'll understand visually and verbally".

"That sounds a little too good to be true," said Chris sounding skeptical.

After grabbing a bite to eat, Simon showed the others where to lay their heads down and then led Chris back to the craft to try and work his magic on the ship's computers.

As they walked up the ramp to the ships entrance, Chris paused for a few seconds. After a sharp intake of breath, he stepped inside. The first thing that he noticed was how clinical everything looked.

When you think of alien ships in sci-fi movies, they are generally dark and scary places with pipes and wires hidden behind grated panels, but here there were no panels, no grates and no doors, everything just seemed to blend and flow. The dull silvery walls were smooth and blended into the floors and ceilings almost like it was a single moulded piece. Simon led Chris down a corridor, passing several rooms to emerge into a central chamber. In the center of the chamber there was a sort of island with screen panels, and in front of that was a large chair and some flat stools coming out of the floor.

"Please, take a seat," said Simon.

Chris tentatively sat down on the stool, and as he did, it began to mould itself around him like a hi-tech armchair.

"Oh shit. ... What the hell's going on?"

"Calm down. It's OK, it's just setting itself for you. It's like liquid metal with intelligence. Mental or what eh!"

"You're not kidding," replied Chris, startled and a little anxious. He looked down at the console, and as if by magic the computers language now appeared in English.

"Fuck me this is so cool! I'll call you if I get anything, OK?"

"Ok. They'll be a couple of my guys on board with you should you need any assistance. I'll catch up with you a bit later. Have fun."

With that Simon left him to it and went off to try and grab a few hours' sleep. He'd been up for some time now, and no doubt tomorrow was going to be another eventful day.

Several hours passed by as Chris delved into the ship's software with relative silence as most of the makeshift camp slept.

Suddenly the sound of distant explosions filled the air, waking Simon and the rest of the camp. Quickly he made his way to the command structure, which housed a radio set-up and various other pieces of technology. Several of the resistance were already monitoring the situation by the time he got there.

"What the fucks going on?" Simon demanded to know.

"From what we can make out," said one of the men, looking up from the radio, "the Gozians have attacked Teemor, and they are holding the Myciens fully responsible for the death of the Gozian we killed yesterday. They've sent in several attack ships and are now in the process of deploying ground troops, and they seem to be advancing in this direction"

"Why would they do this for one guy?" asked Simon.

"Well from what we could make out, the Gozian you killed was the brother of general kulos."

"Oh shit! He's practically royalty! We're in trouble now then. How long before they get here?"

"According to our resistance groups, they've already taken the main town, and there about an hour or so away from us and moving this way in force."

"Shit! Ok," said Simon. Start evacuating everyone; Tell them to use the tunnels that we discovered at the edge of the camp and head north. Avoid contact and keep radio silence until we contact them. What's happening with Chris?"

"I'm not sure. Last time I checked, he had made some progress but that was a while ago."

"Ok. Let's go! Times against us, so let's move."

5

Fleeing for their lives

Simon left the command structure and ran towards the ship, followed by several of his men. The camps alarm had now been activated, and instructions went out to the gathering crowd of resistance fighters. In all the kerfuffle and confusion, Sabrina had also made her way to the entrance of the ship, but was being refused entry by two of Simon's guards.

"What's going on" Simon asked her.

"They won't let me in. I need to be with Chris."

"I'm sorry but this is not a good time. You need to go with the others now!"

"She stays with me," Chris declared. He had come out of the ship to see what all the fuss was about.

"I'm sorry, but we don't have time to discuss this. She goes with the others. Have you made any progress with the computer yet?"

"Maybe... but I'm staying with Sabrina, so if you wanna know, then you'd best let her in."

"Fine! Let her pass, we don't have time for this now. Tell me what you've learnt."

Chris explained that unfortunately the software is heavily encrypted with a cipher which was protecting its systems. "This makes it extremely difficult to crack the access passwords, but luckily, I've managed to isolate one of the subsystems and gained access through a hole in the programming."

"You mean like a back door?"

"Yes exactly. In theory if I can shut down and reboot the system, it should revert back to its original spec, which would be pre-password, allowing me to set a new password and give you full access to the ship."

"Then what are you waiting for? Do it!"

"You don't understand. If I do this, you may lose all the access you've already gained. There are no guarantees that this will work."

"We have no choice, the Gozians will be on us shortly. If we don't try, we will be captured and lose the ship anyway and most definitely our lives. Now do it!"

Chris led Sabrina and the others to the main chamber, sat down, and imputed the shutdown command.

One by one the instrument panels shut down until there was darkness and silence. Seconds later it all sprang back into life.

"What happened? Did it work? What have we got?"

"Everything! We have everything. Defense, offence, shields, engines, we have everything" said Chris excitedly. Sounds of jubilation and happiness filled the air, but the whoops of delight were cut short as the force of an explosion on the edge of the camp sent shock waves throughout the ship that felt like a small earthquake.

Seconds later one of Simon's men came running in to the ship. "You need to get the hell out of here right now!" he screamed.

Simon grabbed hold of him by the shoulders to try and calm him down "What the hell is going on?"

"The Gozians are attacking! They've found us. You must leave now" he repeated frantically.

"I thought you said they were an hour away"

"When you shut the ship down, it dropped our force shields long enough for them to get a lock on our location. They're shooting at us from orbit, and their short-wave attack craft are on route as we speak

"Shit! Chris fire up the engines, and bring up the shields. Everyone else hold on; we're taking off while we still can."

"Simon, I don't know how to fly this thing," said Chris sounding extremely concerned.

"You don't have to. Just do as I say, and I'll take us up. OK?"

Chris looked a little shocked, but there was no time to be squeamish. Simon tapped some commands into the panel, and several seats and anchor points materialized. More explosions could be heard close to the camp, and through the view screen, Simon's resistance fighters could be seen scattering to the edges of the force shield. The door closed, and a blue glow surrounded the ship. The next boom that could be heard was the sound of the engines bursting into life.

"Ok, it's now or never. Hit the power button to your right, and let's get the fuck out of here," said Simon pointing to the instrument panel.

The craft responded immediately, and they began to ascend rapidly, leaving the campsite and Forrest far below them.

Everything seemed to be going to plan when suddenly they were hit by a blast from above, knocking out the navigation and main control panel

Many of Simon's men who had boarded the craft were immediately pinned to the floor with the gravitational force of the ascent as the craft began to gain speed. Sabrina, Chris, and Simon were locked into their seats, unable to move, held in place by the restraining straps.

"Do something. I can't breathe," spluttered Chris.

But Simon was unable to comply and there was nothing he could do to slow the ascent. The craft continued to ascend at a rate of knots, and as they passed through the atmosphere and into space, it collided into a large Gozian carrier ship orbiting above them. There was an almighty explosion which sent Simon's craft spinning out of control until it eventually slowed down and began to drift aimlessly in space.

As Simon looked around, he could see that Chris and Sabrina were still locked in their seats, limp and unconscious. And the craft was rapidly filling with Smoke. The Gozian vessel, although much larger, seemed to have suffered extensive damage to its stern. Through the viewscreen Simon could see that the impact had ripped a hole in its engineering section, and it was now drifting towards the planet below.

Simon struggled frantically to try to release the clamps that were holding him in place, as the air was now becoming toxic from the thickening smoke, which was causing him to choke. As Chris inhaled, the smoke in his lungs caused him to cough, which woke him up. His immediate reaction was to hit every button he could see on the life support panel in front of him. They could hear the air being sucked out of the ship, and the smoke quickly cleared and was replaced by clean breathable air. Once life support had been stabilized, the energy restraints that had held them in their seats were released, and all three of them fell to the floor.

Chris still coughing and trying to catch his breath crawled over to Sabrina. She wasn't breathing! In a blind panic, he attempted to perform mouth-to-mouth resuscitation on her, which he had been taught several years ago whilst on a scuba diving course. After what seemed like an eternity, and to his amazement, her body spluttered into life.

"Thank god, thank god!" Chris kept repeating whilst clutching Sabrina tightly in his arms.

"Wha... What happened?" she asked.

"It's OK, don't talk. We... had an accident. Well, I think it was an accident. There was an explosion, and we lost control. The next thing I remember was waking up with the ship full of smoke."

"An explosion?"

"Yes, I think we hit something."

"Your right! We hit a Gozian ship," said Simon as he struggled to his feet, a little shaken by his ordeal.

"Simon, are you OK? How do you know that we hit a ship?"

"I saw it with my own eyes, and if you look out of your main viewer, it looks like it's about to burn up on its forced re-entry. We need to get this thing operational before we get any more unwanted guests! You'd better check to see who's still alive."

The collision with the Gozian carrier had temporarily curtailed the attack, although everyone knew the respite would be short lived.

* * *

"We have to go now!" Elle screamed at George, who had been knocked to the ground by the last blast that had impacted the campsite.

"Get up," she screamed, grabbing George's arm to pull him up.

George eventually scrambled to his feet. Still quite dazed, he stumbled forward and followed Elle to the edge of the campsite.

"What's that" said George pointing upwards.

The dark night sky was suddenly lit up by an explosion high in the atmosphere. Elle looked up and cried out and the tears began to fall down her face.

"What is it? What's wrong Elle?" Pleaded George.

"Oh shit no! Please, God, don't let that be Simon's ship!"

"Elle you've got to pull yourself together, there's no time! We don't know for sure it was his ship... Elle!" George shook her and slapped her face. "Pull yourself together. We are in grave danger here. I need your help" He got ready to slap her again.

But before his hand could make contact, Elle grabbed his wrist and twisted his arm behind his back. "If you ever do that again you will be very sorry, I assure you." She whispered in his ear before releasing her grip.

George turned to Elle and gave her a hug. "I'm sorry sweetheart but I had to get you focused. Now, can we go?" he said kissing her on the forehead.

"Ok follow me" she said wiping a tear from her eye.

"Follow you where? We are already at the edge of the campsite, and there's nothing but dense forest in front of us"

Elle smiled and lifted her right arm, and it became immediately apparent to George that she had a similar wrist device to the one Simon wore. She pressed a series of buttons and several openings appeared in the ground.

"Quick everyone down here," Elle shouted out before making her way into one of the entrances and down into a dimly lit tunnel, followed quickly by George and many others.

Elle and George scurried down the long dark, muddy tunnel for what seemed like hours, but in reality, it was more like five or six minutes.

Eventually they emerged into a large circular room with what looked like high concrete walls, lit up only by a circle of illuminous stones positioned in the center of the room.

George stopped in his tracks to look around and take in his surroundings. "Wow! This place looks like a scene from the Raiders of the Lost Ark movie"

The stones in the room resembled a place he'd once visited in England called 'Stonehenge,' and in the center of these stones stood a huge concrete slab balanced on two brick pillars. This was obviously some sort of altar.

There were no other entrances or exits to the room than the one they'd just passed through, and when he looked down at the floor of the room, it became apparent that it was covered in detailed stone carvings.

Seconds later the peacefulness was shattered as resistance fighters began pouring into the room. Elle rushed to the altar. She knew it wouldn't be long before the Gozians would be upon them.

"What are you doing" asked George as he followed close behind her.

"Stand back from the walls" she bellowed out.

She began pressing several points on the surface of the altar stone, and suddenly the floor shuddered, and the grinding sound of metal gears whirring could be clearly heard. The room began to rotate in a clockwise direction, revealing several new exits and concealing the original entrance.

"Ok! Everyone down the tunnels now!" screamed Elle.

It didn't take long before the room fell silent again.

"C'mon Elle! What are we waiting for? Let's go!"

"No, we can't go yet. I must conceal the exits before the Gozians blast their way through to protect the resistance"

George wasn't happy but Elle re-activated the altar anyway, spinning the room once again until there were no exits or entrances available.

"Oh, that's just great! Said George sarcastically. "What the hell do we do now? I really don't feel like being a martyr today, Elle!"

She just smiled and told him not to worry. She explained that this was a site-to-site transporter, and it would take them to the neighboring planet Fedora. From there they could take the Sky Lift and get the hell away from all this shit.

"A site-to-site what? And what the hell is a Sky Lift?... and why didn't we all go this way?" asked George who seemed more confused than ever.

"We didn't have the time to take everyone. Everything else I'll explain on the way. Now stop whining and stand next to me OK!"

Elle then attached a device to the altar and inputted her final sequence. There was a flash of light and seconds later the pair of them materialized in the middle of a clearing surrounded by trees in the center of a similar stone structure.

George fell to his knees and began vomiting and complaining of dizziness.

"Yeah, I know. Sorry about that, but it takes a bit of getting used to. Dematerializing and rematerializing takes its toll on the human body, but it was a necessary evil."

"Oooh, I feel terrible," complained George.

"You're so funny" she replied pulling him to his feet.

"C'mon, babe, we're safe for now, but times not on our side."

"Will they follow us?" asked George.

"Not from there. I set an explosive charge on the altar before we left, but it won't take long for them to work out where we've gone.

Elle took George's hand and led him through the trees. The air was different here; it smelt fresher and seemed a little easier to breath. As George looked around, he had the feeling of déja vu, it reminded him very much of his home.

"So, you didn't say what this Sky Lift thing was?"

"It's a little technical, but basically, it's a physical link between the ground and an asteroid in space, sort of like a big elevator. Hence the name 'Sky Lift'.

Ten minutes or so past by, and they eventually emerged from the forest and then followed a path down into a busy marketplace.

"C'mon, it's this way," said Elle. She grabbed George's hand and dragged him past dozens of market stalls that lined the busy street, selling everything from carpets to electronics and of course food of every description. The aromas that filled the air were intoxicating.

"Can't we just get something to eat? I'm starving," George pleaded.

But Elle was having none of it, and she carried on regardless, dragging George behind her.

As they turned the corner, a huge building came into view that looked a little bit like a massive old railway station with the Eiffel tower sticking out of the top of it, rising up into the clouds above.

"Wow, that's impressive! How does it work?" asked George.

As they climbed the steps to the building, Elle explained that they drew energy from the planet's core to power it. They entered the building, and like the market, it was also full of people trying to purchase tickets and queuing up to enter the Sky Lift.

"What now?" said George. "It'll take forever to get to the front of that queue."

Elle pushed past the queue of people, much to their disapproval and approached the security that were guarding the entrance to the Sky Lift.

"Oh, shit, now we're done for," George said under his breath.

"Don't worry. I've got this" Elle replied.

She lifted her top to reveal a tattoo of the sun and the moon combined together surrounded by stars, and the guards immediately ushered her through.

"It's ok, he's with me." she said as George followed close behind her.

They walked through the doors, found a couple of seats, and sat down together.

"How long will this take? And what should I expect when we get there?" asked George.

"Well, it takes about 30 minutes to reach the asteroid, it's been colonized into a sort of space port. I have some connections up there that will help us."

"How is it that you and Simon have all these connections? After all, you haven't actually been here all that long yourselves?"

"You ask far too many questions," said Elle.

6

Seeking Sanctuary

With a clunking sound, the seats upper framework slowly settled over their shoulders like a fair ground ride and locked them into their seats. Some oxygen masks dropped down in front of them, followed by an announcement over the Tanoy.

"Place your masks over your face and relax. The lift will be leaving shortly. Thank you for traveling with 'Sky Lift.'"

This was followed by a buzzing sound, and the lift soon sprang into action and began to ascend.

"So how come you and Simon never got together romantically as a couple?" asked George "You both seem pretty close?"

Elle paused for a moment.

"What's up? is there something between you? I don't want to step on anyone's toes."

"Well... when we took over the ship, Simon and I did become very close." Said Elle "We were all very elated about having got the better of our captors, and in the heat of the moment we did embrace and almost kissed each other"

"It's OK, I don't need to hear anymore. It's really none of my business," said George, sounding quite jealous.

"No wait, let me finish. I shouldn't really tell you this, but I guess you'll find out soon enough."

George reluctantly sat back and listened to Elle's tale.

She went on to tell him that after they'd managed to land the ship, they went through it in search of technology and weapons that might help them.

As they searched Simon stumbled across a hidden compartment which he then opened. Inside of it he discovered a young woman in her twenties submerged in a white liquid with tubes inserted throughout her body that were obviously keeping her alive."

"Really! So, what did you do?" asked George.

"Simon called out with excitement for the rest of us to join him and to help free her from this sticky liquid. Her body retched as he pulled the tubes from her throat, and for a moment it seemed like she wouldn't survive.

"But Simon wouldn't give up on her. After he gave her mouth-to-mouth resuscitation, she spluttered into life. He stayed by her side night and day until eventually she regained consciousness.

Elle told George that his obsession with her ultimately put pay to any possible romance between them. He had become infatuated with the woman, and their connection grew stronger and stronger."

"And that didn't bother you?" asked George.

"No of course not! I think the world of Simon and hold no malice towards either of them; quite the opposite. I wish them all the happiness that they can find."

"So, if you don't mind me asking... where is she now?"

"It turned out that she was of royal blood. She was a princess from the seventh colony, Lunaria."

George just sat there in amazement at what he was being told. Elle then went onto tell him that the princess had been kidnapped in an attempt to blackmail and influence the Lunarian royal family.

She had a hatred towards the Gozians and all they stood for since she was a child.

Once she had sufficiently recovered from her ordeal, she returned to reunite with her family. There she tried persuading her father, the king of Lunaria, to make the Gozians pay for what they did, as she believed that they were ultimately responsible for her abduction.

Elle went on to describe the Gozian race for George in a little more detail.

They were ruthless people, and they believed that they were the master race. They could control the mind, and like the Myciens, they have no respect for any other race. The Lunarians on the other hand were the complete opposite: they were a compassionate and peaceful race who generally fought for what was right. They had a strong connection to nature and were capable of manipulating lunar and solar energy, which they used to power their lifestyle and of course weapons and technology They were more than capable of defending themselves, and although there was a lot of contempt and hatred between the two sides, up until now both sides had been reluctant to go to war with each other. Still, many people were constantly trying to provoke this, and the princess was one of them for obvious reasons.

"I take it the princess helped Simon set up the resistance then. So, what's her name?"

"Her name is Princess Helaine; Simon calls her his lady of the moon. Their relationship is not known about within her family, as her father would undoubtedly disapprove!"

"Well given the tension between the two races that's understandable I guess," said George.

"Enough of that now; I've said too much already. We'd better put the masks on. Otherwise well both pass out through a lack of oxygen before we get there," said Elle smiling.

They both sat back in their seats and relaxed for the rest of the journey. Time past by quickly, and before they knew it the Sky lift began to slow down and eventually drew to a halt as it docked with the meteor. George glanced out of the view screen of the Sky Lift in amazement at what he saw. It was nothing like he'd imagined. The whole place as far as the eye could see was lit up like a Christmas tree and covered with buildings of all shapes and sizes.

"Wow! I keep saying this, but that really is an impressive sight, it's like a screen shot from a sci fi movie," he said in total amazement.

Another announcement came over the Tannoy: "Please depart from the forward doors. We hope you enjoyed your trip, and once again, thanks for traveling with Sky Lift."

George and Elle made their way through the exit and into the main complex.

"What now?" asked George.

"We need to get to docking bay number nine. Simon has set up an exit strategy in case of emergency's just like this."

"what's at docking bay number nine then?" asked George.

"That area is Lunarian territory. We'll be safe there."

"So, the tattoo?" asked George inquisitively.

"The tattoo is a pass from Princess Helaine. It buys me favors from the right people."

"But if the wrong people see that on you, I'm guessing it could have dire consequences."

"Babe... in life you have to take chances if you want to open new doors to achieve your goals. Now c'mon, that's enough chat. Number nine is just over there."

The two of them ran towards the entrance gates, but as they approached, they were stopped in their tracks by several heavily armed men dressed in black uniforms.

"Stop where you are! you are under arrest for murder, terrorism, and crimes against the Gozian state. Drop to your knees, and put your hands behind your heads," he barked at them.

Elle turned around to look for an escape route, but two more guards approached them from behind. They were outnumbered and out of options! They had no choice but to comply.

As they dropped to their knees, the first guard grabbed Elle by the hair and threw her face down on the ground, put his knee on her back and began to handcuff her. Elle cried out in pain; her face was badly cut and heavily bleeding. Seeing this was too much for George to take, and he struck out at the guard to get him off her. Their reply to this action was swift: the sound of gunfire split the air, and George cried out as bullets ripped through his leg and abdomen. Elle screamed out at the guard begging him to stop, but the guard just laughed and pressed down harder on her back.

All the commotion had alerted the Lunarian security, and they arrived at the gate in force, outnumbering the Gozians three to one.

"Stop what you are doing! This is Lunarian territory, and you have no jurisdiction here," One arriving officer demanded.

"Back off Lunarian scum. This is not your business. These two are wanted for terrorism, and we have a warrant for their arrest."

The Gozians drew their weapons, but before they could act, the Lunarians responded in kind, and a fire fight began, resulting in all but one of the Gozians and several of the Lunarians being shot dead.

The remaining Gozian threw his weapon to the ground and surrendered. "This is an act of war!" he protested

"The act of war was committed by your state not ours!' the Lunarian officer replied. "Now take this piece of trash into custody" he commanded his security guards.

The Gozian was promptly led away at gunpoint, and Elle and George were escorted into the main security building. There George was patched up by the doctor to stop the bleeding, and he then rejoined Elle in a holding cell to await interrogation. George was obviously in a bad way, and Elle held him in her arms, still bloodied from her own ordeal.

"Why did you do that?" she sobbed, brushing the hair from his face.

"I've only just found you; I can't lose you now!" she said as the tears rolled down her face. "Don't you realize I'm falling in love with you."

They heard approaching footsteps, and cell door swung open. To Elle's surprise, Princess Helaine walked through the door flanked by several bodyguards. Elle's face lit up, and she ran over to Helaine and threw her arms around her, much to the bodyguard's dismay.

George who was still conscious, looked up at Helaine. She looked every inch of the princess that she was. She stood six feet tall, slender, and of course she was extremely beautiful with long flowing blond hair that had been partly platted on one side. She was of course dressed in the finest of clothes, but the most striking thing about her was her eyes: they were yellow in color, and they had an almost hypnotic sparkle to them that practically drew you in.

"It's so good to see you Elle. What are you doing here? And where's Simon? She asked in a soft, gentle, yet concerned voice.

"I could ask you the same question. Teemor has been attacked and overrun with Gozian soldiers. We had to flee for our lives! I'm really worried about Simon; he escaped in the ship, but I don't know if he's OK. There was an explosion in the atmosphere," she said sobbing.

Princess Helaine's face dropped, and her eyes watered. She took in a deep intake of breath and looked up at Elle. "The situation is far worse than you realize. In the last twenty-four hours the Gozian elite soldiers attacked the royal palace. We managed to drive them back, but my parents were killed in the crossfire. We are now at war with the Gozian empire, and I've mobilized our army accordingly."

"Oh, Helaine, I'm so sorry."

"There's no time for me to grieve right now. We are in the process of evacuating all Lunarian citizens and sympathizers from Fedora as we speak. ...I see your friend has been injured"

"Yes, he was shot outside the gate trying to protect me," said Elle.

"On my ship, the Aurora we have a Kelisi healer. We will take him directly to her. She will repair his wounds."

Princess Helaine turned to her guards and ordered them to take Elle and George to her personal medical bay at once. She also instructed them to scan Teemor's orbit for the possible wreckage of Simons ship.

True to her word, George was rushed to the medical bay with Elle by his side, where they wasted no time in cutting away the clothing that was obstructing his injuries.

After several minutes of cleaning and bathing his wounds, the Kelisi healer walked into the medical bay. She was dressed in a long white gown with her hair tied back, revealing a pale flaky face. "Stand clear," she ordered, and after injecting him with a colored liquid, she hovered her palms over his wounds.

A blue glow seemed to be resonating from her hands, and George's face tightened up, followed by the arching of his back and the obvious discomfort that he was experiencing as if he were getting an electric shock. Elle was looking a little concerned, and if it wasn't for the miracle that was happening before her eyes, she would have certainly intervened.

As she watched in amazement, George's skin seemed to be knitting its self-back together. Within no time at all George's injuries looked fully healed and the Kelisi removed her hands, leaving George to relax back down onto the table where he lay.

"Now you will need to relax," the healer said in a strong, confident voice. "you've been injected with nanomites, which have now been activated. They are repairing your body from within, and it will take some time for your body to adjust."

"Thank you! Thank you so much!" said Elle to the Kelisi as she left the room.

* * *

Back on Simon's ship, things were going from bad to worse.

Several hours had passed by since the collision. The Gozian carrier ship had managed to stabilize its orbit with the help of two other smaller attack craft, although it still had very little propulsion, and one of the attack crafts was now on an intercept course with Simons disabled ship, which apart from life support was basically dead in space. Only a handful of Simon's resistance fighters had survived the ordeal, and most of them were carrying injuries of some sort or other. The medical bay had been destroyed by the original blast from the Gozian carrier, which ironically caused the collision on their own ship by shorting out the electronics on Simon's ship. There was a breach to the outer hull, and they were venting air at an alarming rate.

The Gozian attack craft arrived at Simon's location and began scanning it for survivors. A red light quickly swept through the ship, and seconds later Gozian soldiers began appearing all over the ship.

"What's going on?" cried Sabrina.

"Whatever you do, don't resist," said Simon "just do as your told,"

But the remaining resistance fighters panicked and took up arms against them. It didn't take the Gozians long to kill them all, and once the threat against them had been dealt with, they entered the bridge and surrounded Simon, Chris, and Sabrina at gunpoint.

"Target acquired, three to beam out" said the lead soldier into his communicator.

But as he gave the command, several explosions could be heard outside of the ship.

"We are under attack," came the reply.

"Transport now," demanded the soldier.

A white light filled the room and Simon, Sabrina, Chris, and the Gozian soldiers were all transported off the ship, which exploded soon after due to the impact of the external explosions.

Chris, Sabrina, and several Gozian soldiers rematerialized onto a Lunarian battle cruiser, and the Gozians were quickly dispatched. Sabrina held on to Chris tightly, and they both closed their eyes in anticipation of their own demise, but to their surprise, the lead soldier welcomed them with open arms.

"Come with us," he said.

They were led out of the room and taken to the crew quarters, where they were given fresh clothing and allowed to get cleaned up before being escorted to the bridge, where Elle and George were waiting to greet them.

"Oh my god!" said Chris "We're so happy to see you guys." "How the hell did you manage to find us? Where's Simon and who are your friends?" asked Sabrina in a torrent of words.

After a lot of hugging and kissing. Elle filled them in on what had happened to them and the situation with princess Helaine's family, the declaration of war, and the history between Simon and the Princess.

"So, what's happened to Simon?" asked Chris, sounding very confused. "We thought we were being taken into custody to be tortured or killed, but we ended up here?"

"Helaine's crew located Simon's ship signature, and she'd sent this battle cruiser in to intercept and extract him and anyone else left alive on board. We volunteered to come along to assist in any way we could. The Lunarians tapped into their transport beam and diverted it on to her ship, but unfortunately, Simon was transported onto the Gozian attack craft, which was now on route to rejoin the rest of the Gozian fleet, and it would be suicidal to chase after it, or their cruiser would be destroyed.

"Princess Helaine has had to return to Lunaria" Elle explained, as her planet is under attack, and we are now retreating to a safe distance while they try to locate Simons exact position. The crew on this ship are under strict orders to bring Simon back alive if at all possible."

Once they'd reached a safe distance they managed to pinpoint exactly where Simon was being held. It was in a brig on a small attack craft called the Astonia, which was in orbit over the planet Teemor. It was manned by approximately thirty crew members and surrounded by a force field, so it would be impossible to beam him out.

The only way to retrieve Simon now would be to mount a direct attack by boarding the Astonia, and that could be suicidal.

"Is there any way we can get on board without being seen?" asked Elle.

"There is a slim chance," said the Lunarian Captain. "We have a prototype shuttle on board with a cloaking ability, and it's also equipped with a shield dispersal device. But it's not been tested in battle yet, and if we get caught it's certainly no match for the Astonia."

"If there's even a small chance of success, then I think we should go for it," said Elle "I know princess Helaine would want us to try."

"Ok, I will assemble a team of six of our best soldiers and yourselves, of course, and we will prepare the shuttle for departure."

7

The Reunion

Elle, George, Chris, and Sabrina followed the Lunarian commander down to the shuttle bay, where they were equipped with weapons and protective clothing, and they boarded the shuttle with the six Lunarian's. The pilot ignited the engine and activated the cloaking device, and they set off towards the Gozian ship.

"When we reach the Astonia, we will have to decloak the shuttle to be able to use the shield dispersal unit," said the first officer "This will allow us to get through their shields. From that point on we will be visible to them, so we'll have to move quickly."

"So, what's the plan? What do we do from there?" asked Elle.

"We will beam on board and head to the brig. You will need to shoot on site! They will do the same. Once we get there, we free Simon and make our way back to the beaming point, transport to the shuttle, and get the hell out of there as quick as possible."

"Well, that doesn't sound too bad," said George sarcastically.

"Ok here goes. Is everyone ready?" asked the first officer.

Everyone picked up their weapons and stood by ready for transport. The pilot dropped the cloaking device, passed through the shields, and activated the transporter beam.

As they materialized in the corridor of the Astonia, they heard heavy footsteps, and then two Gozian soldiers appeared with weapons in hand.

The lead Lunarian soldier, Captain Marcus Reed, reacted first. Firing two rapid blasts, he quickly dispatched the Gozians.

Marcus's headphones then crackled into life, and the sound of the pilot's voice burst into his ears.

"Your presence on the ship has been detected. We are moving out of the shielded area to recloak. Contact us when you're ready to depart, over."

Suddenly, alarm sirens blared, and the blue strips along the center of the walls began to flash intermittently.

"Ok, let's go! This blue strip is a motion detector, so we need to move quickly," said Marcus as he began to advance down the long curving corridor.

Everyone else filed in behind him, with the remaining Lunarian's taking up the rear. As they rounded the corner, they could see several doorways towards the end of the corridor.

"The last door at the end is the entrance to the brig, "so let's get it open and get inside" But as Marcus and the others approached the doorway, they heard the familiar sound of heavy footsteps behind them once again.

"Everyone take cover and get ready; this is going to get messy. Chris, you're the tech guy, so get that door open ASAP," said Marcus.

As the Gozians came into view, a gunfight ensued. Flashes of light flew backwards and forwards as Chris desperately tried to override the electric door lock to the brig.

"Get that fucking door open now! Or this mission is over" screamed Marcus.

In the heat of the battle, they manage to take out several Gozian soldiers at the cost of only one Lunarian and a few flesh wounds. Then suddenly, the Gozians gunfire ceased.

"I've got it!" said Chris "The doors open."

But as they began to move into the brig, two silver balls the size of a cricket ball were thrown towards them.

"Go Go-Go!" Screamed Marcus.

Elle led the group through the doorway, but before all the Lunarian's could enter the room, the silver balls let out a piercing sound which dropped the last two Lunarian's to the floor. Marcus quickly shut the door, leaving them where they'd fallen, reeling in agony with their hands desperately clutching their ears.

"What are you doing?? We need to help them!" George shouted at Marcus.

"There's nothing we can do for them," said Marcus "the devices will burst their eardrums and cause their brains to haemorrhage within seconds, and if you step out there now, you will die with them"

"But there your men."

Marcus grabbed George and pushed him against the wall, anger in his eyes he said. "Do you think I'm happy about losing my men? They are my friends! I have to live with that for the rest of my life! Don't ever think that I don't care! I have a job to do, ok?"

"Let him go!" said Elle grabbing hold of Marcus's arm. "Our fight is out there, and our mission is in here!"

Marcus reluctantly released George and recomposed himself. "Right, let's get this done," he said as they moved towards the cells.

In the holding area there were two main cells, one of which was full to the brim with around thirty prisoners, all looking pretty dishevelled. Their clothes were dirty and torn, and it was clear that they had been severely beaten. But seeing Marcus's group come around the corner had had an immediate effect on their moral. Opposite their cell and in complete contrast was another cell of similar size. It was completely empty apart from some electronics and a metal framework that had been set up behind the glass which held Simon for all to see. His face was covered in blood and his eyes were blacked and bruised; it was clear that it was only the framework that was stopping him from collapsing on to the floor.

"Oh my god!" screamed Sabrina. "We have to help him."

Chris began to work on the door lock to Simon's cell.

At the entrance to the brig the Gozians were trying desperately to get in. Suddenly George turned and walked towards the entrance with a fixed look in his eyes as if he was a man on a mission.

"George what are you doing? "Asked Elle, looking confused.

But George pushed past her and reached up to open the door. Seeing what was unfolding, Marcus raised his pulse riffle and fired a shot towards George. Luckily, Elle had anticipated what Marcus was going to do and punched George in the face, knocking him to the ground before the gunshot could hit him. Unfortunately, Marcus had managed to hit the release button instead, which opened the door lock anyway and allowed the Gozians entry to the room.

Chris had now managed to gain access to Simon's cell, and with the help of Sabrina, they'd released him from his shackles.

"Release the other prisoners," were the first words out of his mouth.

"It's ok Simon. We've got you now, but unfortunately, we don't have enough room for everyone on the shuttle."

"Release the prisoners," he demanded. "I will not leave this place without them!"

"You'd better do as he asks," Chris said to Sabrina as she helped Simon to the floor.

The Gozians had now entered the room, and once again a gun fight ensued. Marcus's remaining men managed to take out a few of the Gozians, but there were far too many, and they were soon overpowered, leaving Marcus no option but to surrender and throw out his weapon.

"Lock this scum up and kill their leader. Show them what happens when you defy us!" Snapped the nearest Gozian.

As they approached the cells, the prisoners began pouring out and ran towards them.

"Open fire!" screamed the lead Gozian soldier.

The pulse rifles cut the initial prisoners down with ease, but the prisoners just kept coming and eventually overwhelmed the Gozians. They suffered heavy casualties, but they didn't seem to care. Elle watched on as the remaining prisoners picked Simon up and carried him out of the room past the mass of bodies that now lay on the floor before them.

"Oh my god! I've never seen anything like that before, have you?" said Sabrina.

"No" Chris replied. "I can't say I have. It's almost like he's some kind of God to them! It's like... like a cult or something," replied Chris as they followed the dozen or so remaining prisoners out of the brig.

As Marcus went to walk through the door, Elle blocked his path with her arm. "If you ever take a shot at George again, I'll kill you on the spot!" she snapped.

"He was under the influence of the Gozians. They'd taken over his mind. I had no choice!"

"You might leave your men to die, but we don't do that. Don't ever raise a weapon to us again"

"You cheeky bitch, I'll ..."

But before he could finish his sentence, George stepped in and separated them.

"Hey! I'm the one that was clumped here. Look, he was only acting as he was taught. We're not here to fight each other, so let's get out of here first, and we can deal with this another time, alright?"

Reluctantly they separated and followed the rest of the group back to the beam-out point.

Marcus recalled the shuttle, and although it was a little cramped, they managed to beam out all the remaining survivors of the ordeal and headed back to the Lunarian ship before reinforcements could arrive.

The shuttle docked with the Lunarian ship, the Amelia, and once everyone had embarked, the captain set course for Lunaria.

The prisoners from the Astonia were led to the medical bay to be assessed and nursed back to health. Simon was taken for the first of several sessions with the ships Kelisi healer.

Princess Helaine's ship, the Aurora, already had a head start on them and was the fastest in the fleet. It would take the Amelia at least a week longer to reach the Lunarian home world.

Meanwhile Chris was assigned to engineering to learn more about the technology of the day, and Sabrina volunteered to help out in the medical bay. Elle and George were introduced to special ops training and grew ever closer. The dispute between Marcus and Elle was left unresolved and had been brushed under the carpet for now.

After ten days of traveling, everyone was eager to depart and to get boots onto terra firma. Space was a cold place, and although the Amelia had an adequate heating system, the experience of traveling through space felt very soulless and clinical. There's nothing like the smell of fresh air and the feeling of solid ground under your feet to bring you back down to earth.

The best view from the ship as always was from the bridge, which was surrounded by wraparound panoramic windows.

As the Amelia approached the border, it was clearly visible that a battle of some kind had taken place here, with bits of space junk and debris drifting about aimlessly.

The border effectively consisted of multiple lighted beacons stretching as far as the eye could see, encircling a huge, illuminated planet.

The captain gave the access codes, and a number of beacons switched off, allowing them passage through. At last, the Amelia finally pulled into one of the many docking bays over the planet.

Once assembled, the crew and passengers began beaming down to the surface for some well needed RnR.

Chris, Sabrina, Elle, George, and Simon were ushered onto a waiting shuttle with Marcus and several of his officers. The shuttle took off and headed down towards Kelsha city, which was the capitol of Lunaria.

The planet was effectively built in two halves. On the ground there was a bustling town centre with shop after shop, restaurants and every other establishment imaginable, most of them practically spilling across the pavements. It was like a cross between a posh outlet centre and a thriving marketplace, and like any city, there were roads to control the traffic. The only difference was that, instead of driving on wheels, they hovered above the ground. Advertising smart boards were everywhere, selling a wide range of products. They locked onto anyone who gazed upon them and seemed to talk directly back at you.

The other half of the planet was situated above them, but due to a force shield you could not see anything of it, just a projected image of the perfect day with the sun beaming down. After about twenty minutes the shuttle passed through a tunnel that had been carved into the mountain side and eventually landed onto an artificially lit platform, before being elevated to the upper level. Ten minutes later, the darkness of the elevator shaft was replaced by a flood of light as the Lunarian sun's rays streamed through the shuttle's windows.

Unlike the city below, the land in front of them was very green, fertile, and uncomplicated by roads and commerce. There were no shops or industry, just forests and fields as nature intended. The shuttle lifted off and soared into the air above the vegetation which seemed to come alive, with animals climbing through the trees and scurrying along the ground as they were spooked by the sound of the shuttle's engines.

In the distance they could see a large complex built into the hillside which surrounded what looked like a huge castle.

"I'm guessing that's the palace," said Sabrina.

"This place is beautiful" replied Chris.

"Above ground is the throne room," said Marcus, "as well as our religious facility's, stables, accommodation chalets, spa, et cetera. There are also several restricted levels beneath the ground which hold our fleet command, nobility, and science departments."

"How can all this land sit above your capitol city" inquired Sabrina.

"There's a kind of gravity belt that separates the upper and lower levels of lunaria," said Marcus "It's like two opposing magnets, and it causes the upper level to hover. It's a naturally occurring event, not man-made, and there is of course a forcefield protecting its stability,"

"But I felt the warmth of the sunlight below," said Sabrina.

"The sky and weather projections are controlled to help the lower city thrive," said Marcus.

The shuttle soon touched down in the palace's courtyard, and the doors sprung open. They were met by a contingency of guards who escorted them towards the palace's entrance.

As Simon looked around, it was plain to see that this fairy tale-looking palace had been violated. Although ongoing repair work was occurring, the scars of the recent battle were clearly visible. Scorch marks from small arms fire and several broken windows gave away obvious clues to what had happened here.

"How is Princess Helaine holding up" asked Simon.

"She's putting a brave face on things, but she only buried her parents a few days ago. She's heartbroken inside" replied Marcus.

"So... what happened here? How did they get through?" asked Simon.

Marcus told Simon that a peaceful meeting was being held between Lunaria and the Gozians, and as we were not at war at the time they were in a low state of alert and weren't expecting any aggression. Unfortunately, the Gozians had other plans. While the meeting was taking place, they disabled our defences and general kulos and a contingency of his soldiers beamed down into the palace, and the carnage began. By the time they'd managed to take back control of the situation, our sovereign and many of the palace guards had been killed. Kulos and his men beamed back to his ship, and the battle above the planet began"

"Yes, I saw the debris as we entered your planets orbit. At least you managed to push them back and stop them in their tracks"

"General Kulos knew exactly what he was doing. He didn't attack with his full force; this was a distraction to disable us while they took control of Teemor and the lucrative Mycien slave trade."

"I thought the Gozians and the Lunarian's had an understanding. It doesn't make sense," said Simon.

"There was a military coup and general Kulos took control. His views are much more radical than his cousins"

"That's not good! He has a grudge against me," said Simon.

"So, I've heard. You're high up on his most-wanted list."

"Yes, we disrupted his dreadful slave trading, and in the process his brother was killed."

Marcus led them through the palace entrance, past the glorious spiral staircase, and through several corridors until they eventually reached a large room made up of blocks of weathered stone. Marcus hovered his hand over a switch plate that had been embedded into the rock, and the floor rumbled as the blocks of stone reformed themselves into a stairwell heading down towards the lower levels.

The stone stairwell took them down into a large reception room where refreshments and food had been laid out for everyone.

It wasn't long before the doors to the room burst open, and Princess Helaine and her entourage of bodyguards, diplomats, and maids waltzed in.

Helaine walked over to Marcus and thanked him for his part in the rescue and then made her way over to Simon and threw her arms around him.

"I thought I'd never see you again," she said through her tears.

"You can't get rid of me that easily, sweetheart. I'll always be with you. I love you; you're the only thing that keeps me going."

"I've missed you so much," sobbed Helaine as she held him tightly in her arms.

"I heard what happened to your parents. I'm so sorry baby. Together we will make general Kulos pay for his treachery."

Simon dried her eyes and brushed the hair from her face.

"You need to be strong now, more than ever, for yourself and especially for your people. You're their Queen now."

"Not quite; we haven't had the coronation yet, and now is not the time. I have to make a live announcement to my people shortly. Would you like to join me?" asked Helaine.

"I'm not sure how your people and generals would feel about my presence with you," said Simon.

"I don't care! As you said, I'm their queen now! You complete me, and I want you there. Besides, an introduction from me will boost your popularity, and we need all the help we can get right now," she said, looking straight at Simon.

"You know I can't resist when you look at me like that," said Simon, "but it could lead to repercussions from the Gozians."

Princess Helaine's smile lit up her face. She thanked Simon, kissed him, took him by the hand and led him away to make a public address via the media of television.

As promised, she introduced Simon as one of her allies and vowed to take revenge for her parents' assignation. Simon in turn appealed for everyone, no matter what their race, to rise up against the tyrannous Gozians, to defeat them and to end the cruel slave trade across the galaxy.

From the television studio they went on to a meeting with Helaine's generals to discuss a plan to defeat General Kulos's army. It wouldn't be long before he would turn his attention back to Lunaria, especially as Princess Helaine had now publicly associated herself with Simon and his rebels.

It had been a long day for both Simon and Helaine, and all that was left to do now was to retire to her quarters for some private time together, where they consummated their love for one another.

In the early hours of the following morning Simon and Helaine were awakened by one of her maids.

Their presence was requested immediately by Marcus and Helaine's generals in the war rooms.

Once dressed they headed down to operations.

"What is it? What's so urgent?" asked Princess Helaine.

"You both need to see this" replied Marcus.

As they turned to look at the monitors, they were surprised to see an armada of ships just outside the boarder.

"Are we under attack? Mobilize the fleet immediately" Helaine demanded.

"Our fleet is already in orbit, my lady, and no, we are not under attack. These ships are here in support of us. They say they want to join the rebel alliance. Your joint broadcast seems to have had the desired effect."

Simon opened a channel, welcomed their presence and thanked them for their bravery. In return he was invited onto the lead ship to officially take command of the fleet.

Princess Helaine issued orders to replenish their fuel, food, and water supplies, and at Simons request, they had several cloaking devices installed on the largest ships.

Within forty-eight hours the fleet was at full strength, and as prepared as they could be for what was undoubtedly to come.

8

A Katarian Encounter

Princess Helaine received a message from general Kulos himself. He had obviously seen the broadcast from the Lunarian media.

The message was a warning. Lunaria was to hand over the rebel leader Simon Chambers or face extreme consequences. If they did not comply, they would advance on Lunaria with their full force, which now included Mycien ships and soldiers. It would-be all-out war!

Princess Helaine's response was to say, "We will hand you nothing but the bitter taste of defeat."

Both Helaine and Simon new that Kulos's response would be to advance on Lunaria, and it would be a matter of days before his army was on their way.

"I need to leave with three of the smaller ships," said Simon. "Kulos will be preoccupied with his fleet, and it will be a perfect opportunity to hit him where he's not expecting it,"

"What do you mean? Hit him where?" asked Helaine

"I've been given information on the location of a Gozian outpost where they are building their ships."

"But couldn't you send someone else and stay by my side?" pleaded Helaine.

"You know I'd love nothing more than to fight by your side baby, and once this is done, I will, I promise. This action that I take will weaken and divide his fleet. Don't worry, my lady of the moon... I'll be back before you know it. I love you."

"I love you too" she said hugging him as tightly as she could.

Simon had the Lunarians install cloaking devices, and their latest weapons on the three ships, and after an emotional goodbye, he set sail for Gozian space, taking Elle and a dozen resistance fighters with him.

The Gozian outpost was about seven days travel at full speed, and by the time they would arrive, General Kulos would already be on his way to Lunaria. So, it was imperative that they got there and back as quickly as possible.

While Simon headed off, Helaine's fleet prepared for battle by reinforcing the border defences with attack capabilities. and of course, working and planning with her fleet and her newly acquired friends the rebel resistance as they were now called.

The week soon passed, and as Simon approached the Gozian outpost, he could see, on the long-range scanner that as predicted, the Gozian force were indeed on route to Lunaria.

Like Lunaria, the planet was protected by a formidable forcefield as well as two large defence ships in orbit of the planet. As Simon, Elle, and the third ship approached, they noticed that there were two moons orbiting the planet. The moons had been industrialized and were obviously being used to construct ships and weaponry, and what looked like a mining operation.

Attacking the main planet would be too risky, if not impossible or suicidal, so the obvious targets were definitely the surrounding moons. This would still be a risk, but a much safer option for them.

And so, it began...

Under Simon's orders the third ship decloaked and opened fire on one of the defence ships, causing considerable damage judging by the explosions on its hull. They were obviously not expecting an attack, and by the time they'd responded with attack drones, the third rebel ship was able to spin around and head in for a second attack. This time wasn't quite so easy though, as they were now being bombarded by laser fire from both the drones and the weapons from the damaged ship. Also, the other defence vessel had now responded and was heading toward the situation. Realizing what was about to happen, Simon broke radio silence to warn then, but the crew knew this would be the case and carried on regardless. They managed to get their second set of missiles off, but by now the defence craft was on top of them, and seconds later the drones cut them to pieces.

While their attention was being drawn, Elle and Simon decloaked and began their decent towards the mine, firing pretty much everything they had at the surface below, before heading back up towards the second moon to try and take cover. The missiles impacted the first moon, causing immense damage to the mining operation, destroying everything in their path in a huge ball of fire that could probably be seen from the planet below.

This action had obviously got the attention of the defence force, and they wasted no time in deploying the drones toward Elle and Simon's ships.

"Time to cloak the ship, Elle" said Simon over the radio.

But as Elle tried to engage the cloak, a drone managed to get through and damaged her capability's. "I can't cloak the ship," came the reply.

"Don't worry. I'll de-cloak and transport you out of there," said Simon.

But as he did so, he was also hit by a drone strike. They were both now in trouble and had no chance of either out running the multiple drones that had been deployed, or the defence craft that was closing in on both of them.

"Elle... were not going to make it! Set your ship on a collision course with the manufacturing site on the moon in front of you and I'll do the same. See you on the other side Hun, ...It was a pleasure knowing you."

"It was an honour to be your friend." Elle replied.

Simon headed for the second moon on what they knew would be a suicide run, but it was the only thing left for him to do. If he turned tail and ran, the chances were he wouldn't be able to outrun the Gozian defence craft anyway, and even if he did manage to escape, then this journey would have been a waste of time, and Elle and the other crew members would have died in vain. He had formed a strong bond with Elle and cared for her deeply, so in his mind the right and honourable thing to do was to go down fighting.

The drones and defence ships didn't take too long to catch them up and began showering them with laser shots.

Seconds later there was a huge flash of light above them, followed by a shockwave that disabled not only Simon's and Elle's ships, but also took down the drones and rendered the pursuing Gozian defence craft powerless.

Simon looked up in confusion through the ships windows and was surprised to see Helaine's battle cruiser, the Aurora, above him. The cruiser transported Simon, Elle, and their crew members onto the bridge, just before their ships collided with the moons manufacturing plant. Then the defence cruiser, which was now powerless to stop, crashed, causing significant damage to the second moon. The other defence ship was only just beginning to regain power and was in no position to pursue the Aurora as it turned, recloaked and began to head away from the destruction that they'd left behind them.

Waiting to greet them was Marcus. "What the hell?" Simon asked. "I wasn't expecting you! What's going on?"

"Well, someone had to save your ass. Princess Helaine said you might do something reckless. I had orders to shadow you and intervene only if necessary. That seemed like an appropriate moment," Marcus said laughing.

"Thanks for the rescue," said Elle begrudgingly.

"Look I think we got off on the wrong foot. Truce?" said Marcus.

"Truce... and thank you" she replied, shaking his hand.

"Now let's get the fuck out of here, and back to where the action is," said Marcus.

But as he gave the order to engage the hyper drive, the ships functions shut down simultaneously, and the Aurora was plunged into darkness.

Marcus, Elle, and Simon looked up as a huge metallic structure passed overhead, blocking their view to the Gozian outpost and blotting out the light from the two moons.

"What the hell is that?" asked Simon "Is it Gozian?"

"No... it's too big!" replied Marcus, looking confused. "I've never seen anything like this before."

A humming sound began to emanate from the craft above, followed by a pulse wave which rendered everyone on the Aroura unconscious.

An hour later and Simon finally began to regain consciousness. With his ears still ringing he slowly opened his eyes. He wasn't able to get up straight away. Still dazed and aching all over, he managed to regain his focus.

The large structure that was blocking their view earlier had now disappeared, and the darkness was replaced by a bright light that was radiating from the Gozian planet.

The other feature that Simon instantly noticed, was a ring of rocky debris around the planet. This was similar to the famous rings that surrounded the planet Saturn. This wasn't there before.

The rest of the crew slowly awoke, and fortunately, apart from a few minor injury's where people had fallen and a bit of disorientation, everyone seemed to have survived the ordeal.

"What the hell happened? Said Marcus, still dazed and confused.

"I was hoping you'd tell me that" replied Simon.

Marcus sent a couple of his crew to the engineering bay to install the reserve power crystals so that he could reboot the ship.

Once installed, the Aurora's systems started to come back online. The hyper drive and several of the ships minor functions had suffered some damage, but they were able to quickly get basic propulsion working, and Marcus immediately put the Aroura back into a stable orbit above the Gozian planet.

The remaining Gozian defence ship was still in a disabled state and was no threat to the Aurora at this stage.

Marcus performed a scan of the area to try and explain what had happened.

Sensors showed distressing results, which Marcus doubled-checked just to make sure. The two moons were gone! ... Blown into oblivion, this explained the debris ring that now surrounded the planet.

"This can't be right" said Marcus, sounding really shocked.

"What's up? What can't be right?" asked Simon.

Marcus looked at Simon and the others. "There's no life left on the planet! It's been stripped of all its resources and is basically burning! Its uninhabitable!"

"How is that possible? It had a forcefield protecting it and everyone that inhabited the planet. How is that possible?"

"This is genocide! There's no other word for it."

Marcus then turned to the remaining Gozian defence vessel and scanned it to find out their situation.

The ship was basically intact, although like the Aurora, its power was drained. In contrast to the planet, the ship's crew were all still alive.

"It will only be a matter of time before they are able to reboot their ship, and you can bet that they'll be extremely pissed off and hostile once they realise what has happened here," said Simon.

"Your right," said Marcus; "I think it's time we got the hell out of here." He set the long-range scanner and was distressed to find a large object heading in the general direction of Lunaria.

"Shit! Are you thinking what I'm thinking?"

"That could be the planet killer." Replied Simon. "we'd better get a move on, or Lunaria could suffer a similar fate. We need to warn them! Is the hyper drive online yet?" He sounded distressed.

"Yes, it's just come online, and you don't have to tell me twice..."

Marcus engaged the drive and set it to full speed, and they left Gozian space with as much haste as they could muster.

As they flew through space, Marcus and Simon kept a close eye on the super structure. It didn't seem to be traveling with any urgency, and as a result of this it wasn't long before they were able to catch up with the hostile vessel.

Marcus immediately raised the forcefield around the Aurora.

As they passed the craft, they were scanned, but no action was taken against them. It would seem that they either didn't consider them a threat, or they simply had no interest in them.

Once they'd made enough progress and had put some substantial distance between them, Marcus ordered his engineers to analyse the data from the pulse beam that disabled them earlier, so as to work on a defence against it.

"So, who the hell are they, and why did they attack the Gozian outpost?" asked Simon.

"Well actually, we've made some ground on that front. The

Aurora automatically records movement on its short-range sensor array. We've reviewed the footage of the super-structure just before it disabled us." Said Marcus, "The bad news is that it's a Katari vessel!"

"Who are the Katari? I've not heard of them before," replied Simon.

"The Katari live on the far side of our galaxy, and they are the first colony. We don't have anything to do with them. They are a very advanced race and not very friendly. I am aware that they trade with the Gozians on occasion, amongst others. Normally weapons, energy crystals, et cetera," explained Marcus.

"Well, judging by the fact that we're still alive, I'm guessing the Gozians have definitely pissed them off," Simon stated.

"Well, I'd love to ask them why, but apart from the fact that they generally communicate telepathically, they wouldn't respond to me anyway, as I would be considered as being beneath them. The only person they may respond to is the Princess herself."

"They sound like a barrel of fun!" replied Simon sarcastically.

"There's no compromise with them. Whatever the Gozians did, they're in for a heap of trouble now."

Marcus pushed on at full speed, and after what seemed like a lifetime, they eventually reached Lunarian space.

He dropped out of hyperdrive, cloaked the ship, and headed towards Lunaria, where they found the full force of the Gozian fleet just outside the border beacons. The sky was full of Mycien and Gozian ships of every shape and size.

Inside the border sat the Lunarian Fleet, backed up by Simon's rebel alliance in a sort of Mexican stand-off.

Several of the beacon lights switched off, and the Aurora crossed the borderline, swung around to face the Gozians and decloaked.

The Amelia also decloaked, and Princess Helaine immediately

beamed aboard the Aurora's bridge.

Her eyes lit up when she saw Simon, and she ran into his waiting arms. "Hello gorgeous, did you miss me?"

"I'm so glad to see you, and yes... of course I missed you."

Simon held her in his arms and kissed her while caressing the soft skin on the back of her neck, and running his fingers through her long, silky hair.

"You know..., I'd forgotten how beautiful you are. My heart always beats faster when I'm in your arms."

"I love you Simon, and I hate it when you're not by my side."

"Wherever I am, you'll always be with me, right next to my beating heart" said Simon as he kissed her again.

"I could hold you forever, but I suppose we should deal with what's in front of us. So, bring me up to date, what's been happening here? It looks like you've got your hands full."

"You could say that. So how was your mission? Was it a success?" asked Helaine inquisitively.

Simon explained what had happened at the outpost and told his Lady of the moon that the super structure was heading this way, probably following the Gozian fleet.

"We don't have any dealings or problems normally with the Katari," said Helaine.

"That may be the case, but whatever their beef is with the Gozians, it's going to unfold in Lunarian space, which will undoubtedly draw us into the conflict."

"General Kulos has asked for a face-to-face meeting to discuss our surrender. He's given us twenty-four hours to respond, or he will begin his attack. Time's nearly up"

"Accept his request to talk, and invite him onto the Aurora. I'll stand by your side in the meeting" said Simon smiling.

"That will enrage him; he wants you dead. I can, however, set up frequency blockers to disable all pulse weapons in the meeting."

"That's fine, I'll tell him what's coming his way. I'm sure that will change his train of thought, and it may tip the balance in our favour."

The princess agreed to Simon's suggestion and invited Kulos and his protection entourage on board.

General Kulos and several of his guards were beamed directly to the conference room, where Simon and Helaine were waiting with several of her protection officers.

"What is this! I came to talk to you princess, not this piece of trash besides you!"

"You do not dictate terms! And the only piece of trash here, is standing in front of me. Your nothing but a treacherous coward"

"Aww, is the little princess upset at the loss of her weak parents." said Kulos, smirking.

Simon lunged forward towards general Kulos, but before he could lay his hands on him, a flash of light repelled him backwards.

"Didn't your little whore princess tell you about the conference room forcefield? It's designed to separate warring factions so they don't kill each other during talks."

"Your arrogance astounds me! And you'll pay for your treachery," snapped Simon.

"Enough of this bullshit. Hand this piece of shit over to me, and well go easy on your people after you surrender."

"That will never happen," replied Simon with venom. "In fact, what you don't know is that while you were sitting here thinking about how invincible you were, this insignificant piece of trash just took out your entire outpost and mining facility, so fuck you! We're going nowhere; we're here to fight, and I suggest you look behind you as you've got much bigger trouble than us heading your way."

"Enough of this Smalltalk! you've made your choice; now beam us back, and prepare for your demise," demanded general kulos

"Sure, no problem. I'll beam you back personally," said Helaine as she pushed the transporter pad.

Kulos's guards were returned to their ships immediately, but Helaine had other plans for the general. The transporter beam held him in place, slowly pulling his atoms apart, and with nowhere for him to go, it tore him to bits piece by piece.

"What have you done?" said Simon sounding a little shocked. "I mean, I get it, but ... I hope you're ready for the repercussions to come"

"I don't care; I'm glad he's dead. I hate him."

Marcus entered the room to inform the princess that the Gozian command ship had signalled them and were awaiting a response. Princess Helaine and Simon headed for the bridge. "Patch them through, and prepare to raise shields," the Princess commanded.

"Did you really think you could kill me that easily!"

"Kulos... How is that possible? I killed you."

"Nice try Princess, you only killed a double. You certainly have more spunk than your Father had, but you'll have to do better than that. I'll be seeing you real soon."

The coms channel closed, and Helaine raised the shields immediately. "Prepare to attack!" she commanded.

9

Let the Battle Commence

Princess Helaine's fleet was quite formidable, with state-of-the-art vessels loaded with technology, and once the order was given, they began advancing as one unit towards the border forcefield. In front of them on the other side of the planets forcefield was General Kulos's fleet, made up of Mycien attack craft and of course, dozens of Gozian ships, ranging from huge battle cruisers to much smaller attack vessels including the Astonia.

The Mycien ships surrounded the cruisers to form a defensive ring around them, and General Kulos's cruiser ship, the Fedora, which had been named after the trading planet it was built on, sat right at the back and was well and truly entrenched and protected. It would be difficult to reach him, let alone destroy him.

Simon turned to Helaine and asked to be transported onto one of the smaller attack crafts.

"Why? You're safer on here with me," she replied.

"It's not about being safe," said Simon, "If you want the resistance movement to help you, then I need to be with them, I need to be in control of a raiding ship. I will lead the resistance into battle, backing you up as you attack,"

After a lot of protesting, Princess Helaine finally agreed. Deep down inside she knew that Simon was right and would certainly be more of an asset to her leading the resistance vessels, who were on standby, many of which were still cloaked and would add another element of surprise to the battle.

"Oh, and one more thing, George and Elle are going to try and infiltrate the Gozian fleet, to get near to Kulos."

"How will they do that? They'll never get near him; they look nothing like Gozians." said Simon.

"They're in the medical bay as we speak, having some temporary facial reconstruction done," said the princess. "We have a small captured Gozian attack craft in the docking bay, and once they're finished, they're going to take it and try and merge with the enemy's fleet. This is their frequency so please try not to destroy them" she said smiling.

Simon pulled her in close and kissed her. "No problem, and Good luck Princess" said Simon as he turned and made his way to the transporter room.

The Gozians common features included facial ridges that spanned from their ears to their nose, and they tended to have a blue tinge to their eyes as opposed to white.

The females also had much smaller ear lobes. All of them had an in-built arrogance and were trained as warriors from birth, but they all respected their chain of command with total loyalty.

Elle and George's orders were simple: infiltrate, gather useful data, and report back... and if given the opportunity, kill General Kulos.

The forcefield lights dropped, and contrary to General Kulos's ship, the Fedora, the Aurora led the attack from the front, spraying a barrage of drone missiles that peppered the Mycien protection detail, and magnetically attached themselves to the hull plating. Once attached, they blew small holes in the outer plating, causing the ships air system to decompress, suffocating anyone inside. And as a backup to this, the supporting attack craft directed laser pulses towards critical systems, disabling their manoeuvring capability's.

Of course, the Gozians also had damaging weaponry and responded in kind from inside their ring of protection. The larger cruisers had very sophisticated defence systems, but nothing in life was impregnable, and with enough firepower they could be destroyed.

Many of the smaller vessels from both sides took heavy damage from the first wave of attack, and the centre ground fast became littered with space debris from disabled or destroyed ships.

Amongst all the carnage the Gozian cruisers made their move, and the Aurora soon came under heavy concentrated fire as they advanced on Helaine's ship in force.

Simon watched on, waiting in the wings with his vessel still cloaked as his princess bore the brunt of the onslaught. He could clearly see that she was in trouble and feared for her safety. Instinctively he made the decision to decloak his ship

And swooped in behind the attacking cruisers, followed by several other cloaked ships, and they began an onslaught on the cruisers, ripping chunks out of the tail ends of the Gozian craft.

The cruisers were in attack mode themselves, so their defences were at a minimum, as they hadn't anticipated this move.

The first cruiser took heavy damage and immediately disengaged, seeing this, the other cruisers had no option but to also back off and return to the safety of the Mycien protection ring with Simon and his rebels nipping at their heals as they went.

"Woo hoo! Take that you mother fuckers!" Came the cries of delight over the comms.

"Thanks darling; I needed that. For a second there I thought I was a goner," replied Princess Helaine.

"You're welcome sweetheart," said Simon, "but you weren't in any trouble my lady, I always had your back. Now leave this to us and re-join the fleet to recuperate. We've got this from here" He and his followers began mopping up any damaged stragglers that he felt could pose a threat.

Helaine took Simon's advice and retreated behind the planetary forcefield, and once Simon had finished clearing any immediate danger, he also re-joined the fleet, creating a sort of no man's land and an uneasy calm for both sides as they both licked their wounds and recuperated.

For a short while there was peace, and the carnage had subsided, until General Kulos himself broke the silence and began an open broadcast over the airways.

"Lunarian fleet! You have sustained heavy damage and multiple casualties, and your souverain ship has been severely disabled. If you surrender now, you and your family's will not be harmed, and Lunaria will be left intact under Gozian rule. More ships will be arriving shortly, so you have a choice to make. Choose wisely. You have twenty-four hours to decide."

Princes Helaine responded in kind. Incensed at what she'd just heard, she appealed to the Mycien and Gozian forces to either retreat or surrender.

"Your leader, General Kulos, has taken control of your planet after a vicious military coup. He will eventually be held accountable for his actions and tried for his atrocities.

All of those that stand by him will be treated as conspirators. As the leader of Lunaria, I urge you to surrender now, or many of you will die."

Suffice to say, neither side showed signs of retreating.

Marcus then approached princess Helaine. "My lady, you have a private transmission request coming in from Simon's ship."

"Patch it through immediately," she replied.

"We've had a message from Elle and George," said Simon, "It seems that kulos and a compliment of vessels are leaving the battle zone to confront the Katari vessel that's approaching from the rear. George and Elle are going with them as part of his protection force; he will be isolated from the main fleet, so I thought I might go after him,"

"Our long-range scans show heavy reinforcements heading this way." Replied the Princess. "Like them, we need time to regroup and recover. I need you to stay here and help me protect my planet. Kulos can wait; he will have his hands full and hopefully the Katari will do the job for us. Besides I have a plan."

Twenty-four hours passed by in a flash, and as they approached the deadline that had been given to them, Princess Helaine called a meeting with Simon, Marcus, and several of her generals.

"Simon, it's time to enact my plan. I need you to stay behind the forcefield and be ready to assist me if things go wrong, OK, baby, please, just trust me."

"Sure, sweetheart, whatever you want is cool with me. Just know that I love you. Be safe, and good luck," he said, blowing her a kiss.

Princess Helaine ordered Marcus to prepare the prototype shuttle and she headed down to the shuttle bay. She told Marcus, "OK, I want you to take the Amelia, Simon, and several resistance ships and attack the enemy's front line to create a diversion for me."

With that the princess boarded the prototype, and left the safety of the Aurora, and headed out towards the sun that Lunaria was orbiting.

The Mycien and Gozian forces immediately responded by trying to intercept the Lunarian shuttle, but Marcus and Simon got in-between them and opened fire with all they had. This brought Helaine enough time to put some distance between herself and the Gozian invaders. Unfortunately, Marcus and Simon's entourage could not sustain their attack for very long before having to withdraw. And In response to Marcus's short-lived attack, the Gozian and Mycien forces chased them back towards the border and began a heavy attack on the Lunarian ships that were waiting there.

Meanwhile, the several vessels that were pursuing Helaine's shuttle were catching up fast.

But as she approached the suns chromosphere, she suddenly stopped and did an about-turn to face her oncoming aggressors.

Princess Helaine then began an open broadcast.

"You were warned and now you will pay the price as promised." she said in an abrupt tone.

Suddenly a solar flare erupted from the sun and connected with her prototype shuttle, causing it to light up with such ferocity that it almost certainly blinded anyone looking on. The shuttle then sent out a radiated blast that immediately incinerated the oncoming vessels. Surprisingly though, the shuttle itself seemed to be completely undamaged, and it began to speed towards Lunaria and the ongoing battle, stopping just outside the boarder.

Several ships turned their attentions to it and opened fire. But the shuttle was still pulsating with a glowing light, and when the missiles and drone strikes hit the hull, it just absorbed them like they were nothing. Suddenly it began to glow brightly once again and shot out a multidirectional blast that obliterated the several ships that were firing on it. The blast then seemed to expand cutting into the Gozian fleet and causing massive damage to multiple vessels. This obviously had the desired effect, and the rest of the attacking force withdrew to what they considered a safe distance.

Princess Helaine's shuttle then crossed the border forcefield and re-docked with the battle-scarred Aurora, where Simon was eagerly and anxiously awaiting her arrival.

As soon as the air pressure equalized, the shuttle bay doors opened, and Simon rushed in. Unfortunately, he wasn't able to approach the shuttle, as it was still glowing hot from its interactions with the sun.

The shuttle doors opened, and to his relief, Princess Helaine slowly stepped out. Her skin was glowing and had become almost translucent. Her blood vessels and organs were clear to see.

"What the hell is happening?" screamed Simon. "Are you alright? Someone get the Kelisi healer: she needs help now!"

"Do not approach me. I'm still channelling the suns energy and it will kill you if you get too close," Helaine told Simon as she stumbled to the floor.

"Helaine!" Screamed Simon as he reached for her, but the skin on his hands began to burn as if acid had been poured onto them. Marcus and a couple of the crew members restrained Simon and pulled him back.

Fortunately, the Kelisi healer arrived and immediately attended to Helaine. She seemed impervious to the radiation that the princess's body was omitting.

"What's happening? why is she like this?" said Simon.

"She is the lady of the sun and the moon," replied Marcus; "She can channel energy from both of them, as you've just witnessed. But it comes at a cost. She will need time to recover."

Once the Kelisi had dealt with the princess, she sent her to sickbay and then dressed Simons wounds.

A call came in over the radio requesting Simon's presence on the bridge, as they had received a coded message from Elle and George.

It seemed that General Kulos had made contact with the Katari vessel. It demanded settlement for suppling technology that Kulos had used to equip his ships.

As he hadn't made payment on time, he was told to give them the earths location or face all-out war!

The virus that had swept throughout the Gozian empire and other planets, had now reached their planet, and was beginning to destroy their ability to reproduce, so they intended to get ahead of the game and enslave earth to use its inhabitants as surrogates to perpetuate their race.

"This is dreadful news!" Simon retorted. "The only reason I am here fighting this battle is because of my abduction, which was brought on as a result of slavery. Now another master race is considering getting involved in the very thing that I and many others are so opposed to." He turned to walk away in angered frustration.

"Well, I guess we'll have to deal with that issue another day," said Marcus. "At the moment we have our own problems to deal with, and they're in front of us right now. "

Simon turned back towards Marcus and in anger said,

"You really don't get it do you? They are talking about attacking and enslaving my world! Next it will be another and another, and eventually it will be yours! Your wife... your child, sister, or brother. You may be able to defeat them today, but eventually they'll overpower you. The only way to stop them is to change their thought process."

"And how do we do that?" asked Marcus

"How did you become a captain? Cause It certainly wasn't for your intelligence, that's for sure," said Simon sarcastically.

Marcus didn't take to kindly to Simon's wit. He grabbed hold of his jacket, and in anger with his fist raised he pushed Simon up against the wall.

"Go on then! You haven't got the bottle. Your just an uneducated short-sighted soldier, obeying orders without question or thought for the repercussions and consequences of your actions."

Marcus let out a scream in rage and thrust his fist towards Simon's face, catching the side of his head, and a fight broke out between them. As they scuffled at close quarters, the bridge crew ran over to try and separate them. The bridge lift doors opened, and Princess Helaine's personal security detail entered the room and restrained and separated the two of them.

"Arrest this insubordinate fool," Marcus demanded.

"We have orders to place you both in the brig until the princess is able to talk to you"

"What? You can't arrest me... I'm the captain of the guard. I outrank you!"

"But you don't outrank the Princess. and like it or not, both of you are going to the brig to cool off"

Simon and Marcus were handcuffed and escorted to the brig, where they were put in separate cells, much to their annoyance.

* * *

On the Gozian attack craft, George and Elle had been asked to dock with general Kulos's ship to enable it to be serviced, rearmed, and made ready to re-join the attack on Lunaria. This could be the opportunity that they'd been waiting for.

They entered the docking bay and were escorted to temporary quarters, where they were able to get cleaned up and rest for a few hours. They were also told that they could use the canteen, but all the upper decks were strictly off limit.

"I'm going to jump in the shower, as I'm beginning to smell like a Gozian pig," said Elle. "Do you want to join me?"

"Hmm, you know, I'd love to baby, but I'm going to check out the canteen first to see what I can find out." He kissed Elle and headed down the ship's corridor.

He entered the canteen, which was bigger than the inside of his attack craft and full of crew members. It was a very busy room fitted with long tables and a large serving area.

He walked up to the servery and ordered some food from the woman behind the counter.

"Would you like anything to drink?" she asked him.

"Yes please; anything strong and alcoholic will do," said George with a smile.

As George turned to find a table, he collided straight into an approaching female officer and dropped his drink on the floor.

"Oh! I'm so sorry! Are you OK?" she asked, sounding both concerned and embarrassed.

"I'm fine, thanks, and ... don't worry, it was my fault. I should have been looking at where I was going."

"Not really. It was down to my inpatients. Let me get you another one." She beckoned to the waitress and told her to clear the mess up and then to bring another drink over to her table.

"Please join me," she said to George, "at least to eat your food and to wait for your drink to arrive. I owe you that much at least." She pointed over to a small table in the officer's area and led the way.

"So, what's your name? I'm lieutenant Angel Charmers, but you can call me Angel," she said with a flirty smile.

"My name's George. I was just checking out the canteen, but I never expected to run into such a beautiful lieutenant as yourself,"

Angel was quite athletic, stood five feet six inches tall with dark brown hair, and had the usual blue tint to her eyes.

Blushing, she replied, "You flatter me; thank you. So, I don't believe I've seen you before. What's your station?"

"I'm not part of this ship, I was invited on board with my shipmate to recuperate while my attack craft is refuelled and refitted. We are part of the cruisers escort."

They chatted and continued the flirting for the next ten minutes or so while George finished off his food and drink.

"You have very unusual facial ridges," said Angel, "I find you extremely attractive. We should go to my quarters and explore our desires at once."

"Is that wise? Are you not on duty?" George said, trying to deflect her sexual advances.

But she had already made up her mind and knew what she

wanted; she wasn't taking no for an answer. George found himself being led to her quarters and although he was aware of what was happening, he could do nothing about it.

When a Gozian woman was aroused, she would project her thoughts and desires towards her potential mate, and normally if the Gozian male felt the same, they would mate. But if he didn't want to mate, then he would project his decision back to her and could then break the cycle. Unfortunately for George, he was not a Gozian and could not stop what was about to happen.

They entered her quarters and the door closed behind them. her sexual desires completely overwhelmed George. It was like she'd not only taken over his mind but also his body and senses; he no longer had any free will, and his carnal desires went into overdrive.

It wasn't long before they were all over each other, kissing, caressing, and frantically undressing each other. George's heart rate and blood pressure went through the roof as they dropped to the floor with arms and legs entwined. Angel flipped him onto his back and spent the next ten or fifteen minutes making frenzied love to him. There was nothing George could do to stop her; all her feelings and senses were projected into George's mind and body. He had never experienced anything like this before and was powerless to resist. When she was finished, she collapsed onto his naked perspiring body. George couldn't speak and was desperately trying his best to catch his breath.

"Wow! ...that was fantastic! Most guys are a little reserved, but you showed no resistance at all. I really enjoyed that," she said, kissing him slowly on the lips.

Angel climbed to her feet and headed to the shower.

"Join me" she said beckoning to George, who was now only just starting to get his breath back.

Once they'd finished showering and dressing angel poured George a drink and they sat down together around the table in the centre of the room.

10

Repercussions of Infidelity

George was now coming to his senses, as Angel released her grip on his mind, and the severity of what just happened, was now beginning to sink in. In his mind he was now feeling guilt as he loved Elle and would never have done this normally. He was totally devoted to her and was now really annoyed with himself.

"Are you OK?" asked Angel.

George was a little quiet, still contemplating what had just happened. But before he could answer, Angel received a call over her com's device. "Lieutenant charmers, report to the bridge at once. The Katari captain has requested our presence on his ship. Bring two security guards with you."

"Ok, we must go now. You and your shipmate can act as my security; we'll pick him up along the way."

"My shipmate is female, not male; her name is Elle."

"Ok lover, but we need to go now, as general Kulos doesn't like to be kept waiting."

They left her room and headed back towards the crew quarters.

George went inside and quickly explained to Elle that they had been asked to escort General Kulos and his officer onto the Katari ship, leaving out the encounter that he'd just had with Angel. This was not the time to try and explain what had just happened between them. Clearly this might be the opportunity to assassinate the general, or at the very least find out what's going on between the Gozians and the Katari.

"We still need to be on our guard," he said, "as there is the possibility that it could be a hostile meeting that were walking into."

Elle got herself together and followed George to meet up with Angel, who was waiting outside her quarters. Introductions were made, and they were escorted to the docking bay. There they boarded the shuttle with general kulos and two more of his closest security team and headed out towards the Katari vessel, which was docked off the starboard side of Kulos's battle cruiser the Fedora.

The Katari ship completely dwarfed the cruiser in size; it was more like a city than a ship.

"Wow! Look at the size of that thing," said Elle.

"It's not the size that counts, it's how you use it," Angel replied giggling to herself.

"Isn't that the truth? Boys with their toys, eh," said Elle, smiling.

But this was indeed a big toy, and a very dangerous one in the wrong hands. They would certainly need to have their wits about them. As they docked with the Katari vessel, General kulos briefed them on his protection needs and told them to keep quiet during the meeting, but to also be alert to any possible danger, and to be ready to act if absolutely necessary.

They stepped out of the shuttle and were met by a detail of Katari soldiers. They were of normal human size and proportions, but their most striking feature was their faces. They all had dark hair and white skin, but their eyes were what could only be described as lizard like, with eyelids that closed vertically. The light in the docking bay had been dimmed, so it was a little difficult to see clearly, but what they could make out was the gecko look to their skin, blended with smooth clear patches from the nose down. They had a definite reptilian look about them.

They escorted everyone out of the docking bay and into a conference room with a large table surrounded by extravagant looking chairs. General kulos and Lieutenant chambers sat down opposite several Katari dignitaries. The security stood behind the seated areas either side of the table.

After several minutes of uncomfortable silence, the conference room doors opened. A large figure of a man adorned with jewellery around his neck and implanted into his face waltzed into the room, heavily flanked by his personal security detail. The Katari dignitaries immediately stood up and bowed their heads in respect.

General Kulos also stood up and nodded in his direction.

"Be seated for Commander Azrael" he said.

Everyone around the table took their seats.

The desk before each of them then lit up, and a computerized message was broadcasted.

"For the benefit of complete understanding the translator system has been activated."

Then as they began to communicate, the panels in front of each person speaking lit up, and a computerized conversation began.

George and Elle listened intently at what seemed like a heated exchange taking place. It was a bit strange, as no one actually spoke a word; the computer seemed to be reading the thoughts of each of the participants and the translating their thoughts into words. The only way you could tell it was an uncomfortable meeting was from the hand gesturing and angry faces.

It seemed that General Kulos had struck a trade deal with the Katari for technology in return for some sort of weapons-grade mineral. The problem was that in all the haste of the military coup, kulos had used the minerals to make his own weapons and therefore had failed to make payment. The Katari took this as a betrayal; hence their response to the attack on the Gozian outpost.

Neither Kulos nor Azrael was in the mood to back down.

Suddenly commander Azrael slammed his fist down on the table, and his security detail raised their weapons and stepped forward. In response George, Elle, and general Kulos's security did the same. The situation was now extremely tense!

Lieutenant Angel then stepped into the argument. "Look, we had every intention of making payment to you, but you have attacked our outpost at the expense of many Gozian lives! There must be some way we can resolve this matter without killing each other?"

"We will retire and consider your request," came the response from the translator.

Everyone lowered their weapons, and the stand-off was temporarily averted. Commander Azrael and two of his dignitaries stood up and left the room leaving his security detail in place. After ten or fifteen minutes of being kept waiting, General kulos began to get impatient, and Angel tried to calm him down.

"That's it! We're leaving," he blurted out. "If its war they want, then It's war well give them."

Weapons were raised again, but before the shooting began, the conference room doors reopened, and Azrael came back in and sat down with his sidekicks.

"We do not accept any betrayal, and the punishment for this was our attack on your outpost. As for the outstanding payment, this will be made immediately"

"But we've already informed you," said Angel, "that we do not have payment at this moment. We need more time."

"There will be no extensions to the deadline! If you cannot make payment of this type, then we demand an alternate payment."

"What alternate payment are you looking for." asked Angel.

"General Azrael will require the location of the ninth colony, and will take over the lucrative slave trade that you're so heavily involved in."

"This is not an acceptable option!" General Kulos declared. "You have never shown any interest in this trade before; why now?"

"The virus that has made many of your race infertile has now started to infest the Katarian empire, and we need to address this now. This is the only option that is on offer to you; otherwise we will declare war with your race."

"This is outrageous!" said Kulos aggressively.

"We will have a short recess for you to consider this option"

With that Azrael and all his security and dignitaries left the room again.

General kulos was very angry at this request. After an exchange of aggressive outbursts between Angel and himself, they finally sat down to discuss their options.

"I know you don't want to lose the rights to the slave trade," said Angel, "but at this moment we are outgunned outnumbered, and in the middle of an uprising, so our forces are spread thinly. This is something that we can come back to at a later date."

"I know your right, but I hate being dictated to by these inferior lizards! Who the hell do they think they are?"

"Now is not the time. We need to deal with the Lunarian problem first. "Angel pleaded with general Kulos to see sense.

"Ok, we will solve the problems with Lunaria and then regroup and address the arrogance of the Katari full on. For now, we will give them the location that they require"

Azrael was called back into the room, and a second treaty was signed begrudgingly. General Kulos also decided to suspend trading with the Katari for the present moment.

There wasn't really any opportunity for George and Elle to get involved in the decision making or to take general kulos out; as his own security pretty much surrounded him at all times.

As they headed back towards the shuttle, Angel turned to George and said, "Well, that could have turned out a lot worse"

"Yes, but you've just passed on the problem to another unsuspecting race," said George.

"Better them than us. Maybe we can get together again later to celebrate. What do think?"

"Let's get back first," he replied.

"What does she mean by that?" asked Elle.

"I can't talk about it now baby, I'll tell you later; this Is not the right time or place."

"What have you done?" Elle demanded to know. "What happened between you and her?

"Baby, I can't tell you now. Please wait till we get back," he pleaded, stretching out a hand to calm her.

"Don't you dare touch me!" she said angrily.

No other words were exchanged between them on the journey back. The atmosphere between them was very frosty.

Once they docked back on the Fedora, George and Elle returned to their quarters and were told to prepare to disembark within the hour as general kulos had decided to return to Lunaria as soon as possible.

George then set about the unenviable task of telling Elle what had happened between himself and Angel, without being too explicit. Surface to say, she didn't take the news very well. Her initial reaction was to slap George around the face.

"How could you do this to me? I thought you loved me! I guess that was all bullshit! Your no different to everyone else" she screamed.

"Baby, I'm really sorry, but ..."

"Don't baby me! you've broke my heart into a million pieces and shattered my world! I'm not your baby anymore."

"Don't you get it? I couldn't do anything about it; she took over my mind and body. I would never willingly do this to you. I love you. Please forgive me."

"Right! ...I suppose she just fell on your dick did she! Just stay away from me. I don't want to see you, or talk to you right now, OK!" she screamed.

As much as it hurt him, he knew in his heart he had to walk away from Elle. Now was definitely not the right time to resolve this issue between them.

"That's right, fuck off and see your Gozian whore," she shouted at him as he left the room.

George headed for the canteen to get himself a drink.

He took his seat at the servery, ordered the strongest drink available, and knocked it back in seconds. He then ordered another.

He'd only been there a short while before he felt a hand caress the back of his head.

"Evening lover" It was the voice of Angel.

But before she could take it any further, Elle appeared and threw a punch, which hit Angel clean in the face, knocking her to the ground.

"Keep your filthy hands off my man, you fucking slut" Elle screamed at her.

Several security guards rushed over and restrained Elle, forcing her to the ground with her hands behind her back.

"Let her go," George pleaded. "This is a personal misunderstanding ... Please"

Angel climbed to her feet, wiped the blood from under her nose, and then grabbed Elle by her hair. "You'll pay for that with your life," she said.

"Please let her go," begged George. "She's, my girlfriend. She found out about our encounter and reacted with jealousy. If you need to punish anyone, then punish me, Please."

Angel pondered in thought for a few seconds then looked at George. "Go! Leave the ship now. and take this piece of trash with you. When we return to Lunaria, you will rejoin the rest of the fleet, and we'll never speak again" She turned to the security guards. "Escort them to their craft and off this vessel immediately," she commanded.

George looked up at Angel and nodded in thanks. The pair of them were manhandled to their attack craft, and once on board, they left the Fedora's docking bay.

They retook their position alongside the cruiser and awaited further instructions.

"Look" George said, "I'm so sorry! I absolutely didn't want this to happen. There really wasn't anything I could do to stop her. Please forgive me."

"Right now, I don't want to talk about it, OK? Just leave it there and leave me the fuck alone!" said Elle, "You'd better send a message to Simon to let him know what's happed here today."

The connection between them had suffered a major blow, but it would take some time to get back to Lunaria, so an uneven calm was the best that both of them could hope for. In the meantime, there relationship was definitely on hold.

George sent the coded message to Simon, and they waited for their orders to depart.

11

The Battle for Lunaria

Back on the Aurora princess Helaine had now regained most of her strength and entered the brig to sort the problem out between Marcus and Simon.

Marcus bowed his head in embarrassment as she approached his confinement chamber.

"What's going on between you and Simon?" she asked him through the security force shield.

"My Lady, please forgive me. I don't know what came over me. "

"I've seen the footage of what happened between the both of you, and I have to say that if you ever do anything like that again, I will have no hesitation in stripping you of your rank immediately. I expect much more from my officers! Do I make myself clear?"

"Yes, my lady. My apologies. I assure you It will never happen again," Marcus said, still standing with his head bowed.

Helaine ordered her guards to release Marcus and told him to resume his duties on the bridge immediately. Once he'd left the room, she approached Simon's cell. "Deactivate the force field and visibility screen; then leave us." she commanded.

The screen dropped and revealed Simon laying on the bunk with his hands behind his head.

"Are you done? Or am I to stay locked up here for a little longer?" he said in his usual sarcastic tone.

"Who the hell do you think you are" Helaine snapped at him.

"In case you've forgotten, I'm the guy that saved your life and freed you from a Mycien slave ship!" Simon snapped back. "I'm also the guy that's supposed to be your soulmate, so don't ever lock me up or speak to me like a child again. If it wasn't for me, you wouldn't be here at all"

Princess Helaine's eyes welled up, and her stern persona crumbled. "I don't want to fight with you. Don't ever think I'm not grateful to you for all you've done for me. Can we not just get past this incident? I couldn't just confine Marcus; it would have undermined my authority in front of my crew," she said as she sat down beside Simon caressing his face.

Simon had much more to say to her in his head, but he loved her so much and just couldn't stay mad at her for long. He sighed and took her in his arms and embraced her. "It's OK, I'm sorry if I upset you. I'm a stubborn bastard at times. You know I think the world of you; I just get carried away with my emotions and can't stop myself saying what's on my mind."

"Simon, you wear your heart on your sleeve. Your forwardness, honesty, literal thinking, and heart of gold are what attracts me to you." She said as she kissed him on the cheek. "Its why I love you so much and why so many people follow you right now. And talking of people, we still have a battle to win, and your followers are waiting for their leader."

"We best go and join Marcus on the bridge then." Simon replied with a wry smile. "And don't worry; I'll make my peace with him for now ... although I can't promise how long that peace will last."

Princess Helaine and Simon joined the other officers in the conference room on the bridge and as promised, Simon made his peace with Marcus as best as he could.

The current situation had changed quite dramatically. The Gozian reinforcements had just arrived which boosted their fleet by 30 per cent. But on a positive note, another thirty small rebel ships had appeared to support Simon's cause, and several more lunarian vessels had also returned to join in the fight. From the chat that they'd picked up over the airways it seemed that the Gozians were about to attack the border forcefield ahead of an all-out attack, so Marcus had put the whole fleet on high alert with all shields raised.

Simon was given command of the Amelia, and once he'd transported on board, he addressed the independent ships' captains, and everyone took position for the battle that was about to commence.

The Mycien ships moved into point position, followed by an armada of Gozian vessels, from small attack crafts to the Huge Gozian cruisers.

The Amelia and dozens of smaller crafts, backed up by the lunarian forces, sat opposite them on the other side of the forcefield.

Simon then openly broadcasted a message across the airways for all to here ...

"Ok, here it comes. This is for the freedom of all races. If we lose this battle then you, your families, and everyone you know and love will become slaves to the Gozian empire, so I need everyone to be prepared to die fighting, if necessary, to protect the generation that will be here when we are not! Are you with me?"

The response was overwhelming to the point where it actually jammed the airways.

And then it began ...

Simon looked on and waited on his side of the beacons as the Gozian cruisers opened the attack with a series of heavy-duty missiles fired directly at the forcefield beacons in conjunction with laser fire from the Mycien craft that lit up the sky like a major fireworks display.

The beacons were equipped with a Star Wars-type defence system which was designed to shoot down any incoming weapon or vessel and immediately went into attack mode. This high tec system was feared by even the Gozian race, which is why they were attempting to take it out first. Initially the system worked well and caused immense damage to the Mycien attack fleet, which had been sent in closer as their range of fire power was much shorter. But the sheer volume of projectiles and laser fire would eventually take its toll.

As much as he desperately wanted to engage with the oncoming vessels, Simon couldn't do anything to interfere with the bombardment while the beacons were intact and in attack mode. He had no choice but to stand by in readiness for the eventual failure of the beacons.

The attack continued for just over twelve hours before the first beacon failed and was consequently destroyed, leaving a gap in the defence system. Shortly after that, various other beacons were also destroyed until eventually the whole system completely shut down and as predicted, the Mycien attack vessels moved in and headed towards the Lunarian fleet, guns blazing.

Simon's Amelia was the first to respond. He was desperate to get more involved in this battle and drive this barbaric force back where it came from. He was followed closely by his rebel army and immediately clashed with the Mycien crafts.

On the long-range scanners, a large contingency of vessels could be seen approaching from the west. It was unclear to Simon who's side they were on, and it was too late to withdraw now, so he continued his advance on the Gozian forces.

Six ships descended on the Amelia, hitting it with everything they had, completely ignoring the approaching vessels from the west. Luckily for Simon, the Mycien ships were much smaller than the Gozian attack craft, and as a result he only suffered minor damage to his force shield and a few external sensors. Simons rebel army surrounded the Amelia to give it more protection and began to pick off the Mycien's one by one as Simon advanced towards the oncoming fleet.

An exchange of weapons fire between the Amelia and several more powerful Gozian vessels saw the destruction of the smaller independent rebel ships as well as the Mycien craft. Both sides were suffering extensive losses, and as big and powerful as she was, the Amelia also took quite a pounding in the exchange as did the Gozian vessels, with chunks of space debris flying of in all directions. Shields were down to 20 per cent with hull breaches and electrical fires on several decks. Simon was outmanned and outgunned and had untold casualties on board. He'd taken quite a beating.

All around him he could see a combination of Lunarian ships and his rebel fighters ferociously going head-to-head with the Gozian forces.

Simon had made his peace in his own mind with the onslaught that was relentlessly coming at him. He knew in his heart of hearts that there wasn't much hope of victory here, as the odds were far to stacked against him. But he was a stubborn man and believed in sticking to his principles, even if it meant his own demise.

Suddenly from the west, massive weapons fire lit up the darkness, servery damaging the two leading Gozian cruisers, and then dozens of ships moved in on the battle front and pushed the Gozian Armada backwards into a defensive position. For now, at least, the Gozians had been forced to retreat and regroup.

To Simon's amazement, the vessels lined up in front of the Amelia and various other Lunarian and rebel ships to create a barrier between them.

Simon immediately pressed the broadcast button on the consul.

"I don't know who you are, but I just need to thank you for your assistance," he said

"It's OK, Simon," said Princess Helaine. "They are allies of Lunaria. Marcus is going to lock a tractor beam onto you, and tow you back to dock with our repair station to see if we can patch up that ship and get her operational again"

"I thought I was done for there, baby. So, who are these mysterious allies of yours?"

"They are the Kelisi. You met one of them when you were

injured."

"Oh, the healer, you mean?"

"They are not all healers. I'm going to beam you aboard. I've set up a meeting with their leaders, as they'd very much like to meet you."

"What about the Gozians?"

"It's OK, they'll be licking their wounds for some time to come, so we'll be safe for a while."

Simon was transported over to the Aurora with the surviving members of his crew, many of which were taken straight to sick bay. As a precaution Simon was also advised to pay the medical bay a visit for a basic health check.

The first face that was there to greet him was Sabrina. She had been training under the kelisi healer for some time now, and with her history as a nurse, she had become quite proficient at it.

"Hey sweetheart, how are you?" said Simon, smiling. "I've been sent down here for a check-up, but I'm fine really. I only came down here to check up on my crew... and of course, to see you."

"You always were a charmer. Now lie down over there, as I need to check you over. Orders are orders."

Simon lay on the bed, and Sabrina attached a device to her hand and began to run it up and down his body.

"You're getting quite good at that, but I'm afraid you'll only find a few cuts and bruises on me.

"That'll be the nanomite transfusion you were given after they rescued you from that Gozian cell"

"How do you mean?"

Sabrina went on to explain that nanomites were a mixture of technology and living insects which had been genetically enhanced.

Once in one's system, they would automatically be drawn to failed or damaged cells and will consume them, thereby eradicating sickness and illness. The really clever stuff came when the tech was activated in the mites with these hand devices. "They can do many things," she said, "From knitting bones together to slowing down the aging process, even fully taking over the immune system, depending on the skills of the person wielding the device."

"You're obviously a quick learner. So how long will they last in my system?" Simon asked.

"They'll be with you forever! As I said there a live insect. They constantly multiply and are part of your blood stream now."

"So, my body's constantly repairing itself with the help of these mites" said Simon smiling. "I must admit I do feel a lot stronger and healthier, and I'm looking much sexier in front of the mirror these days"

"You keep telling yourself that," replied Sabrina, as she laughed out loud.

Simon got up and gave Sabrina a huge hug and then went around the sick bay checking up on all his crew and thanking them for all their hard work and sacrifice. He then left and made his way back to the upper deck to meet up with Princess Helaine in the conference room, where she was now hosting the Kelisi dignitary's.

As he entered the room, Helaine was quick to greet him, slinging her arms around him and embracing him with a kiss. She then took his hand and walked him towards the Kelisi delegates. Like Helaine's healer, they also had pale, flaky skin with long blond flowing locks of hair draped over the back of the silky coloured garments. It was obvious to Simon that they were from the higher end of society, possibly of Nobel. blood.

"Watch closely, and follow my lead," Helaine whispered to Simon.

She walked up to each of them one at a time and with arms by their sides they turned their palms towards her. Helaine followed suit and pushed her palms against theirs. They both bowed and pressed foreheads together.

Simon followed in Helaine's footsteps, repeating her actions, and once the meet and greet was complete, everyone took their seats around a large oblong shaped console table in the centre of the room.

Simon wasted no time in once again thanking them for their assistance.

"You are more than welcome." The evident leader of the Kelisi delegation replied. "We have been allies to Lunaria for centuries, and Helaine's parents were close friends of ours. the princess informed us of the despicable act that took her parents' lives and asked for our assistance in the turmoil that is upon lunaria as we speak. We are more than happy to assist you in any way that we can."

"And do you all feel that way on your planet? "

"There are always dissenting voices in all societies, but in general and overall, we had no hesitation in coming to your aid."

"So, are you going to introduce me?" asked Simon.

"So sorry how rude of me," said the Princess.

"This is queen Anumara, and either side of her are her children, Prince Reka and the beautiful Princess Alita."

"I'm honoured to meet you, "said Simon.

"The honour is all ours," replied the queen. "You are the future king and husband of Princess Helaine."

"We haven't actually set a wedding date yet," said Helaine, blushing.

"That's understandable under the circumstances but, once all this trouble is over, I'm certain you will. Afterall its clear to everyone, that you are both so very much in love. You radiate with excitement in each other's presence"

Food and beverages were served, and the topic of conversation moved onto the slave trade that Simon was so desperately opposed to.

"We have followed your quest for the cessation of the slave trade that's being perpetuated by several influential races, and we agree with you completely," said Prince Rika.

"In my eyes its totally wrong." Said Simon. "Part of the problem is that this virus that has spread throughout the galaxy has caused an infertility problem, and their answer to it is to imprison women from other races to become surrogates against their will, many of them do not survive the process. It's barbaric, and it needs to stop."

"Your anger and repulsion are clear to see." Replied the prince. "The surrogacy problem does play a big part in driving the slave trade, although it's not the only reason it exists. Fortunately, we are in a position to help with the former."

"How do you mean?" Simon asked. "How can you help?"

Princess Alita went on to explain that the Kelisi had been conducting tests for some time now to try to find answers to the fertility virus and believed that they had now made a breakthrough."

They had a lot of success early on with human DNA mixed with nanomite tech, but in most cases, it soon failed on the female fertility systems.

So, they worked on genetic engineering and modification, and with a mixture of all these approaches, they came up with a solution that they believe will cure up to 90 percent of the infertility caused by this virus."

"That's fantastic news, and it will take away a massive incentive for people to buy slaves. So why don't we announce it," said Simon.

"Now is not the right time or situation. Once this is resolved and the dust settles, we will ask for volunteers to step forward, so that we can remove any doubts that this cure works. Then there will be the matter of cost."

"I'm super excited to hear that, although I would prefer it happens sooner rather than later, but It's definitely a step in the right direction."

"In the meantime, I have a gift for you, Simon" said Princess Alita.

"Should I be worried." said Helaine with a smile.

"No, my lady, I meant no intrusion. I would like to perform an enhancement program on Simon. It will engineer his DNA so that he can also draw on and use the solar energy that Lunaria thrives on."

"Thank you; that's very generous of you. I'd love to accept your gift, said Simon as he kissed the hand of Princess Alita.

The meeting was interrupted at this point by a crew member bringing the news that the bridge was picking up a lot of radio chatter from the Gozians regarding general Kulos's return to the battle. It seemed that the Katari were now also heading this way and had sent some sort of message to general kulos.

"I'm afraid we must deal with this," said Princess Helaine, "so if you'll excuse us, we'll return as soon as we can. Please help yourself to whatever you desire" said Princess Helaine as she and Simon left the room.

On the way to the bridge, Helaine took the opportunity to fill Simon in on the history of their race.

She told him that the kelisi were a very powerful yet peaceful race. They had been a great ally to Lunaria, and they were known for their technical advances. Scientifically they were far ahead of any other species. But they did have quite a chequered past, advancing their society without ethics, and committing what many would say were terrible atrocities along the way on the path to enlightenment, and their present way of life. They were without doubt a formidable force to be reckoned with.

"So, what you're saying is tread carefully." Said Simon. "I understand they're not squeaky clean, and I have to wonder what tests they've put people through to find this fertility cure that they claim to have, and at what cost to the lives of the participants. Still, their discovery could be a game changer, so I guess were stuck between the devil and the deep blue sea here,"

"What does that mean?" asked Helaine.

"It means for now we choose the lesser of the two evils. We need their assistance, so I'll accept their offer of the DNA enhancement. It would be rude not to, and I don't wish to offend them. Now let's see what's going on with these Katarians."

Simon and the princess entered the bridge and walked over to see Marcus at the communications console.

They were informed that general Kulos and his entourage would be back in Lunarian territory within a day. He had been communicating with his forces and had told them to withhold any more attacks until he returned. Also, some sort of coded message had be sent directly to him from the Katari, who were also heading this way.

"Can we contact George and Elle? Asked Simon.

"Yes, I think they are just about in range," said Marcus.

"Send a coded message to them to get in touch as soon as it's safe to do so," said the princess.

"Yes, my lady, I'll inform you once we get a reply."

Simon and Helaine left the bridge and headed back to their distinguished guests.

They updated the kelisi on what was happening, and true to his word, Simon allowed the Kelisi to perform their DNA enhancement on him. This involved him lying down while Alita hovered her device over him. It was pretty painless and not really apparent to him that anything had actually changed, but he thanked them anyway. Soon they re-joined the ship and took a defensive position in readiness of what was to come.

12

A Hollow Victory

Five hours passed by before the call from the bridge came through. Marcus had finally secured a safe connection with George and Elle.

Once they'd got dressed, Simon and Helaine made their way back to the bridge.

"George, can you hear me?" asked Simon.

"Yeah, I read you loud and clear."

What's going on with general kulos? we're intercepting all sorts of confusing messages here."

"We are escorting Kulos back to Lunaria as we speak. We should be back in about eighteen hours"

"So, what's going on with the Katari? I'm hearing something about a second meeting just outside Lunaria; should we be concerned?"

"The first meeting didn't go so well for Kulos and finished with him backing down with a nasty taste in his mouth, so I'm quite surprised that they're meeting again so soon."

"I need you and Elle to get back on the ship and find out what's going on," said Simon.

"Yeah ... that might be a problem!" said George.

"Your damn right it's a fucking problem." came the reply from Elle as she took over the comms from George.

"I'm sensing that the two of you are having a little domestic, and now is really not the time," said Simon.

"Yeah, well, right time or not," Elle continued, "I can't go back on that ship, as I had an altercation with Kulos's second in command and was barred from ever returning, thanks to George and his Gozian whore!"

"What! Put George back on the comms," Simon demanded.

"I'm sorry, Simon," said George, "it's not what you think. Well, it sort of is, but its more complicated than that."

"So, are you able to get back on the ship without Elle?"

"It's possible, but I'd prefer you not to ask me to do that, as my relationship with Elle has taken quite a hit, and that really wouldn't help us."

"I'm really sorry, but I have to ask you," Simon responded. "It could make the difference between our winning and losing this battle, with thousands of lives at risk. I need you to put your domestic issues to one side and do this for me, please."

After a pause, Elle took back the comms. "George is going to try to get back on the ship, but once we are back in transporter range, I want this Gozian disguise removed, so I can be reassigned to another vessel. It's making my skin crawl!"

Simon cared a great deal for Elle and had no hesitation in granting her request. To be fair, he didn't have much of a choice if he wanted to keep Elle on side.

The next eighteen hours passed without incident, and as predicted, general Kulos's ship pulled in behind his forces that were on standby outside the boundaries of Lunaria.

With the help of the Kelisi, the Lunarian engineers had used the opportunity of the ceasefire to repair the defence beacons, which were now fully operational once more.

As promised Simon transported Elle off the Gozian attack craft and left George to work at contacting Angel in an effort to get back onto Kulos's vessel.

In the meantime, Helaine began teaching Simon how to channel the suns energy and to use it to charge the banks in the aurora's weapons array This was a slow process and would take some time to master.

***

The Katari vessel was slowly approaching but stopped short of the battle zone, and a transmission was sent to request general kulos presence asap.

George had been repeatedly sending messages to Angel who had finally decided to reply.

"Why are you messaging me? I thought I made myself perfectly clear! "She snapped.

"Sorry sweetheart, but I've been thinking about you. Elle's been transferred off the ship, so she's not an issue anymore."

"Actually, I might have something exciting to tell you, " said Angel, sounding very chirpy.

"Really? So, tell me now."

"No, I need to tell you face to face. Why don't you come over to the shuttle bay? We have another meeting with the Katari and are leaving soon. You could accompany me as part of the security detail."

George was quick to agree, and after messaging Simon, he headed back onto the Fedora.

As he stepped out of his craft onto the metal grating that covered the floor of the shuttle bay, Angel approached him and before he could open his mouth, she slapped him around the face and then wrapped her arms around him kissing him, passionately on the lips.

"What the hell was that for?"

"You deserved that from last time, and the kiss was because I actually missed you," she said.

"I missed you too, babe. So, what's this face-to-face news that you have?"

"Well, I know it's almost impossible, but I think I'm pregnant! Isn't that great news? If it's true, then I'll be the first Gozian woman to give birth since the virus swept through our race. This is a really big deal," she said brimming with excitement and happiness.

"How would you know so soon? Has the doctor confirmed this yet?" George asked nervously.

"I have hyposensitive interoception, as do most Gozian women. Interoception is the sense of oneself; It's the ability to understand the body's physical signals. It is often known as the hidden sense and is referred to as the eighth sensory system. But I'll go see the doctor to confirm it, once this meeting is done. Then we can announce it to the world."

She was extremely happy, unlike George. How was he going to tell her that he was not actually a Gozian? Once a DNA test was completed, they would know the child was not a pure Gozian, and the repercussions were bound to be severe. Angel led him to her quarters, and it wasn't long before the conversation turned to passion once again.

Within a couple of hours, the call came down to Angel that they would be heading off to rejoin the Katari ship shortly.

Angel and George got themselves dressed and headed back

to the shuttle bay to meet up with general kulos and his personal security detail.

"I want everyone on full alert. I don't trust these reptiles, and I'm not sure exactly why they want to meet us again so soon," said the general.

The shuttle taxied out toward the Katari vessel, and once the force shield had been dropped, it made its way inside.

The general and his security were once again led to the conference room. This time things were a little different. There were no armed security guards, and refreshments had been laid out in advance for them to enjoy.

There were female reptilians, for want of a better word, who were on standby to wait on general Kulos's party while they waited for Azrael to arrive. You could clearly sense a much friendlier atmosphere.

After a short wait, Azrael and a few of his advisors entered the room, refreshments were served, and the waitresses then backed away from the table for the conference to begin.

"Ok ... so why are we here? I thought we'd finalized all our business." was Kulos's opening gambit.

Azrael paused for a few seconds then laid out his plan for the road ahead. Firstly, all attacks on Lunaria were to cease immediately.

Secondly, the Gozian forces were to withdraw and regroup in readiness for a full-scale invasion on the Ninth colony Earth, with the full backing of the Katari ships and their technology.

"The planets resources will be drained to enhance both our worlds, and the population that remains after the invasion will be enslaved." Azrael continued, "You can take all that you need from the planet and population, and we will do the same. This will be a very lucrative enterprise for both our worlds, and we will solve this human issue once and for all. In return we will supply all the weapons-grade minerals that you require to get the job done"

General kulos was a little taken aback by this proposal and none too happy about being told to cease his attack on Lunaria. "That's quite an ambitious plan you have. Why would you want to take so many humans? You're talking about a population of millions! The slave market would be swamped and become worthless. I already have a major force stationed here on the Lunarian border; it's only a matter of time before we defeat them, and I will have taken control of this whole region without having to travel light years across the galaxy."

"The human element is a blight to our society and is already spreading out of control. How much longer do you think it will be before they infest and take over our way of life? They are already causing you problems in the small numbers that are here now. And as far as swamping the slave market, we want them for different reasons. We will not introduce any of the humans that we take to the slave market; that enterprise is totally yours."

"What other reasons would you want them for?" general kulos asked.

"That's on a need-to-know basis and private to us!" Azrael snapped back.

"With all due respect, I need to know; otherwise, we have no deal! You may have a large vessel here, but in case you hadn't noticed, I have more than enough fire power here to combat you if I desire" said kulos in a somewhat threatening manner.

Azrael was visibly annoyed at this response, as he wasn't used to being forced to concede ground on his demands.

Angel quickly stepped into the conversation to block the deterioration of the talks. "Why don't we all take a break to consider our positions on this matter?" she said trying to defuse the situation.

Azrael's advisors also stepped into the talks and convinced him to take a time out to consider his response. They were fully aware of the danger that Kulos's forces represented and the fact that they would need them to accomplish this ambitious plan.

Azrael called a halt to the talks and he and his advisors left the room to privately discuss the Gozians request for information.

George was horrified at what he'd heard here, but was in no position to voice his views, as he would surely be executed if they found out who he really was.

In the break he managed to pull Angel to one side. "Surely he's not going to agree to this annihilation of another species," he whispered in her ear.

"I must admit this is quite a radical and unexpected move, but ultimately it's not up to me, and judging by Azrael's response to Kulos's request, I'm not really sure which way this will go."

But before he could say any more to angel, Azrael once again entered the room. "After careful consideration we have decided to reveal our interest in the population of the ninth colony," said Azrael's advisor.

"Apart from the obvious food source that the humans would provide us, it's come to our attention that a possible cure for the infertility virus that has swept this region and affected so many is on the verge of being completed, but to manufacture enough of the vaccine, we would need to genetically engineer the cure on a huge scale, and for this we would use the human population. That is as much and more than we would like to reveal at this moment in time. So ... do we have an agreement?"

General kulos paused for a few minutes as if deep in thought. He was clearly running all the possible scenarios through his head.

"Ok, we have a deal! I'll have my advisors draw up a written contract outlining the proposal and a list of all the minerals and weaponry we'll require between us to achieve this invasion. Also, we would want to benefit from this vaccine at no more than a minimal cost to us. And in the meantime, we will withdraw and begin our preparations."

"Excellent! A toast to our newly formed alliance," said Azrael, raising his glass with a contented look on his scaly face.

George's heart sank as the realisation of what had just been agreed sunk in. Reluctantly, he raised his glass with the others in the room, but secretly felt horrified and just wanted to get the hell out of there as quickly as possible.

"Well at least that's settled," said Angel excitedly. "And we can now return to Gozia and spend some quality time together. I'll arrange the doctor's appointment to confirm this possible pregnancy as soon as we get back." But George was in no mood for excitement. He felt numb and sick to his stomach.

The meeting concluded, and the Gozian party headed back to the shuttle bay and left to redock with the Fedora, Kulos's flagship cruiser.

Shortly afterwards the Katari vessel left the vicinity.

* * *

Back on the Aurora, Marcus sent a message requesting Simon and the princess's presence on the bridge.

As they entered the room, they could see through the giant view screen the beginnings of a mass withdrawal of the attacking forces that previously stood before them.

"What's going on?" asked Princess Helaine.

"I'm not sure, my lady," replied Marcus. "Kulos's shuttle returned from the Katari vessel and gave the order to withdraw"

"Where are the Katari?"

"They have also left my lady. What are your orders?

"It seems the battle is over, but stay on high alert," said the princess "I don't trust the Gozians. Contact the Kelisi to see if they can shed any light on what's just occurred,"

The Kelisi confirmed to the princess that the Katari had contacted them to say that they had indeed struck a deal with the Gozian attack force to withdraw and end the conflict. The battle was over. They agreed to stay in Lunarian space until all the attacking forces had left, but essentially the fight was over. It seemed a hollow victory to Helaine, but she announced the decision of the Gozians withdrawal to her fleet anyway, which brought back noisy celebrations over the airways.

"Congratulations on your victory, my Lady," said Marcus, bowing towards her. "Perhaps now we can proceed with plans for your coronation."

"This is great news for you Helaine," said Simon, "but I'd really like to know why they left so easily and what was decided in that meeting. Have we heard from George yet? It must have been a hell of an incentive for kulos to just back down like that. I don't like it!"

Within an hour all Kulos's forces including his flagship, the Fedora had vacated the vicinity with no word from George.

"I'm really not happy about this!" Simon told Marcus.

"Can you not get a fix on George's location tracker?"

"Look its over!" said Marcus "Why can't you just leave it at that? George was obviously a casualty of war. It happens; we've all lost friends and family in this battle. You need to get over it."

Princess Helaine watched as Simon's face turned to rage, and his eyes turned to a glint of yellow. Before anyone could stop him, he landed several punches with extreme force and lightning speed to the face of Marcus, knocking him to the ground and rendering him almost unconscious.

"You insensitive bastard!" he screamed. "George is my friend, and as you've been told before, we don't leave our friends behind."

The princess immediately had Simon escorted off the bridge, while the medics attended to a very dazed and bruised Marcus.

This time, though, to defuse Simon's rage, Helaine decided

to take him not to the brig but to her quarters, where she soon rejoined him.

"Simon, what the hell's got into you? You just hit him with the solar force that's inside you now. You could have killed him. We should be celebrating, not fighting each other," she said as she held him tightly in her arms.

"That guy is the most insensitive dickhead I've ever had the displeasure of meeting and deserved all he got! You should dismiss him at once.

"Look I'm sorry that you feel that way, but he is a very capable and loyal commander who will no doubt have to spend some time in the medical bay now, so please don't ask me to make decisions like that. I love you, but I have a duty to protect my people with the best soldiers I have available to me. I will search for your friend's tracker and help you locate him, OK?" she said, hugging and kissing him.

"Fine ... but don't ask me to apologise this time, because it's not going to happen. Let me know when you get any news about George, please," he said as he tried to recompose himself.

13

The Journey Home

A few hours later, the long-range scanners showed that the Gozian forces were well on their way back to their territory. After they thanked the Kelisi for their assistance, those vessels also left Lunarian space.

An encrypted message had been received from George and had just been decoded. It outlined the points of the agreement between the Gozians and the Katari, and it didn't make pleasant reading for Simon. George was unable to leave the Fedora before they disembarked, but he planned to escape as soon as humanly possible. He said he would contact them when he got close enough to Lunaria.

The Fedora was too far away, and too well protected by its own force field for George's tracker to be picked up, so they had no choice but to wait for George to contact them.

"This is terrible news!" said Simon, feeling distraught, "Earth doesn't stand a chance. My whole planet will be destroyed! I can't stand by and let this happen."

"What are you going to do about it? You cannot fight them on your own," said the princess.

"I don't know, baby, but I have to do something. I'll call a meeting with the rebel forces and throw it open to suggestions. Ultimately, I will have to return to Earth somehow and at least warn them, maybe help them with their defences."

"Look, why don't you sleep on it and deal with it in the morning when you've had time to think about the logical response?" she suggested. "We'll set a meeting up in the morning on Lunaria and discuss the possibilities. You need to rest; it's been a tough time lately, and everyone needs some downtime. It will take months for them to prepare for this invasion, not to mention the journey to Earth, so we have time on our side. OK, baby?"

"Ok ... maybe your right. We'll deal with this tomorrow," replied Simon reluctantly.

True to her word, Princess Helaine set up a meeting the next day. The rebel captains and representatives from the Kelisi race were invited, and the meeting was also streamed live to all the forces stationed in orbit over Lunaria.

The message from George was played for all to hear, and the discussions began. Many suggestions were thrown on the table, from attacking the Katari directly, to supplying Earth with technology to assist them in combating the impending invasion.

The Kelisi agreed to supply some technology, but as Earth had no alliance with them, they were reluctant to get directly involved in the fight. Most of the rebels were happy to accompany Simon back to Earth, and the princess agreed to supply schematics for the defence beacons that surrounded her own planet as well as tech, weaponry, and the Amelia for Simon to get there. She couldn't commit the majority of her own forces, as she had to protect her own planet, and on top of that she still had the coronation to deal with. Although she did give him a contingency of her best elite soldiers to help pilot the Amelia and to fight alongside him, should he require their assistance. She obviously wasn't happy about Simon leaving her but completely understood that this was something that he had to do.

It would take Simon several months to reach Earth's orbit with his followers in tow, and once he'd got there, he knew that he would then have the unenviable task of convincing the planet's leaders to come together, to prepare and to build the defences that they would need, to go some way towards protecting themselves.

This was indeed a tall order and what seemed like an impossible task, but it was one that he had to undertake.

Simon put his crew together, including Chris, who had now had extensive training on the computer systems and engineering. Naturally Chris's partner Sabrina would head up the medical bay. Elle joined Simon as his security officer and second in command should anything happen to him.

There was still no word on George, and unfortunately, they really didn't have time to wait for his possible return, but Princess Helaine said that she would of course watch out for him. Some of Simons rebels would stay behind and try their best to sabotage and delay the Gozian and Katari alliance as much as they could.

Within twenty-four hours of the meeting Simon and his rebels were ready to go, and after a tearful and emotional goodbye between himself and his lady of the moon, they set off on the long and perilous journey back to Earth.

Simon was a little upset about the fact that he would miss her coronation, but he felt that he really had no choice as his hand had now been forced.

* * *

On the Fedora they were traveling at full speed back to Gozia, and George was no closer to coming up with a plan to escape. He knew the clock was ticking against him, but until the Fedora slowed down, he wouldn't be able to leave the ship. Even then, he'd have to come up with a reasonable excuse as to why he wanted to leave without raising suspicion. To make matters worse he'd looked into Gozian pregnancies and found out that the average gestation period for a Gozian female was only 190 days, and angel was already suffering from sporadic morning sickness and was eager to inform the medical staff on board of the possible pregnancy.

George, on the other hand, was doing his utmost to convince her to wait until they returned to terra-firma. He knew that he and

Angel would become the centre of attention once it became public knowledge that a natural Gozian pregnancy had occurred, and he would then get found out and probably be tortured and executed. He had quite a dilemma on his hands.

Two weeks passed by before the ship finally entered Gozian space, and they docked at a huge space station sited just above the brightly lit planet of Gozia. Angel had asked George to stay with her while she went through her pregnancy, but he obviously couldn't do that, even though he'd actually grown quite close to her now, especially with her carrying his child.

George agreed to move in with her but told her that he had to sort out his affairs first, so would meet her later at her address. This was his only chance of getting away. He kissed her on the lips, wished her luck with the doctors, and headed towards the shuttle bay to get to his ship.

As he opened the door to the shuttle bay, he was surprised to be greeted by a heavily armed security force.

"Going somewhere?" they asked.

"Just getting some bits out of my vessel," replied George.

"We have orders direct from general kulos to take you in for questioning," replied the guard.

"Questioning for what? Is this how you treat a loyal solider that's just fought alongside you? This is ridiculous!"

"A coded message sent to Lunaria has been traced to your vessel, so you will surrender your weapon and come with us. This is an order not a request," the guard said in a very stern voice.

George had no options left to him, he knew they would quickly find out who he was, and the thought of being tortured, and no doubt killed didn't really appeal to him, so he drew his weapon and opened fire on the first guard and managed to wound several others before he was subdued and overpowered by the remaining guard detail.

* * *

Back on the Amelia, Chris had got the engines purring at optimal speed as they headed back toward Earth. Most of the crew were in cryo tubes, as three months in space would be extremely taxing on the average human and Lunarian bodies. Simon stayed awake at the helm for the journey as the nanomites in his system, not to mention the DNA enhancement that the Kelisi had given him, had made him a lot stronger and less susceptible to fatigue. Sabrina had the Kelisi device to help her and Chris to sustain the pressures of the journey.

As expected, it took just under three months to reach Earth, and as they settled into orbit, Simon put the Amelia into stealth mode so as to hide the ship away from any radar or satellites, and of course the orbiting space station. The rest of his rebel followers would arrive over the next few days as they weren't quite as fast as the Amelia.

He then triggered the cryo sleep release sequence to awaken the rest of the crew. Elle was the first to appear on the bridge, looking a little woozy from her long sleep.

"Wow, now there's a sight I thought I'd never see again. Isn't it beautiful?" she said, looking at the big blue planet in front of her.

"It is," replied Simon, "but to be honest, I quite like the life I'm building for myself on Lunaria. Don't get me wrong, it'll be good to visit friends and family, but what are you going to tell them about where you've been for the last eight or nine months?"

"That's a fair point, but I'm still pleased to be back."

"Well, I need to contact the Earth's leaders and convince them to work together to save this beautiful blue planet of ours. But your welcome to beam down to visit whomever you like; just don't let them know about us up here just yet, or they'll end up locking you up in the local looney bin." said Simon giggling out loud.

Elle thanked and hugged him and then headed to the transporter bay to beam down to Earth.

Chris decided to stay onboard, as he had some important information he needed to share with Simon. "Whilst I was going through the Lunarian computer systems, I stumbled across some very old schematics in their database on a planetary communications and transportation array," he said

"How will that help us now? In case you'd forgotten, we are in Earth's orbit now."

"Yes, but the schematics also included the ninth colony, Earth."

"How old?"

"Ancient; we are talking about thousands of years, maybe more. The point is, we might be able to reactivate it with your newfound ability to harness the solar energy."

"So, where is it?"

"it's in plain sight and has been since it was built. It's better known as 'Stonehenge.'"

"Of course! That makes perfect sense" said Simon as it dawned on him that it was very similar to the planet-to-planet transporter under the forest on Teemor.

"Once we get to the surface, you'll need to charge the alter stone, and then we can assess its capabilities and see where it's linked to."

"Ok, that's a great idea, we might be able to use that to our advantage when the time comes, but in the meantime, I need to figure out a way to convince the earth's leaders to work together, or we have no chance of winning this impending battle"

Simon decided the best and quickest way to deal with this would be to confront them directly. He also knew that the rest of his fleet of ships would be arriving soon, and unlike the Amelia, they didn't all have stealth technology. That meant that they would show up on earths monitoring systems.

Once the crew had fully recovered from their cryo sleep, Simon gave the orders to lower the stealth shield that made them invisible to onlookers. He then left orbit and headed down into the earth's atmosphere.

"I hope you know what you're doing. This is going to cause mass panic," said Chris.

"I need to get their attention, so I haven't really got a choice," Simon replied. He headed down through the clouds and settled over Stonehenge in Salisbury.

"Ok beam a team down and take out any security. Then set up a perimeter force field. It won't be long before this place will be swamped with people trying to see what's going on, closely followed by the armed forces."

The next thing Simon did was to lock into the satellites above the planet to broadcast a message worldwide.

"You may have already realised a space craft has just arrived from another galaxy and is now hovering over Stonehenge in England. First, I want to assure everyone on this planet that we are not here to harm anyone. In fact, quite the opposite is true. We come in peace with the intentions of protecting this planet. I invite all the world's leaders, from the European Union to the G7 members, NATO, Asia, African and Arab nations, to a world meeting to discuss the protection of this planet. We await your reply ... and be aware that time is of the essence!"

"Well, that should get their attention, "said Chris sarcastically.

Simon knew this approach would probably cause a bit of panic in the world, as there are always conspiracy theorists, but it was the best and most direct approach he could think of. In the meantime, he had to take the prototype shuttle towards the sun's corona to gather the solar energy to activate the alter at Stonehenge; he would also need to bank some power to help Earth construct the weapons that they would need to fight this fight.

Simon was a little nervous at the thought of doing this as he hadn't experienced it yet. And he knew that although he was capable, it would still take its toll on him. Still, there was no time like the present, so he boarded the prototype shuttle and headed off towards the sun.

Chris beamed down to Stonehenge with Sabrina to scan the stones to make sure they could be reactivated. By now a crowd had formed outside the force shield, and the armed forces were arriving on the scene. It didn't take long for them to move everyone back and set up a perimeter ring around the henge, creating a sort of no man's land.

The good news was that the stones still had residual activity inside them.

Simon's shuttle could clearly be seen re-entering Earth's atmosphere, as it was glowing white hot.

"Beam back up to the ship," said Simon to Chris and Sabrina, sounding out of breath.

After they'd cleared the area, Simon directed a solar beam toward the stones. You could clearly see them glowing white hot with the extreme heat, but they didn't melt or distort in any way. And once they'd cooled down, Chris beamed back down to the site, and sure enough, the energy coming from the stones was now off the scales as if fully charged. Also, the centre stone now had a visible panel on show.

Simon re-entered the shuttle bay, and like Princess Helaine, he stumbled out of the vessel and collapsed. Several of the waiting Lunarian soldiers wearing protective suits picked him up and carried him to the sickbay where Sabrina was on standby to help him regenerate and allow him to rest.

In the meantime, down on the ground things were heating up. Negotiator's, scientists, politicians, and the press were eager to make first contact with this mysterious craft hovering over Stonehenge. The prime minister of England was making a direct appeal to talk with the ship, and on top of everything else, the rest of Simon's fleet had arrived. They were now visible above the planet and could clearly be seen by the NASA space station.

The armed forces had already tried and failed to pass through the force shield that surrounded the site and were now frantically working with the negotiators to get an answer from the ship.

Chris left a team of Lunarian technicians to work on the stones and beamed back onto the Amelia to respond to the negotiators.

A meeting was eventually set up in the Farnborough exhibition and conference centre by invitation only for all world leaders to attend.

The press at this stage were not invited, so as to limit any panic that they would no doubt cause by their negative, pessimistic, and manipulative reporting.

They were told that Simon, the ship's captain, and a security detail would be directly beamed into the conference centre to make an address to the world leaders and to answer any questions that they had for him. He would then beam back out and leave them to discuss and decide on what course of action that they'd like to take. They were told that any interference from armed forces or armed bodyguards, apart from the external protection of the building, would not be tolerated and would be swiftly delt with.

It didn't take long for the location of the meeting to get out to the press, as the army were drafted in by their hundreds to protect the venue and all access routes from the airport to the conference centre.

The media circus of speculation began as the world watched on with bated breath.

Over the next twenty-four hours the presidents of the United States, Russia, China and world leaders from all over the globe began to arrive. The media were unhappy that they couldn't get near the venue as a no-fly zone had been set up around Farnborough to discourage any onlookers in helicopters and obviously to protect the dignitaries from all over the world. This was by far the biggest event that had ever taken place on Earth.

14

Forming a Planetary Alliance

The time arrived, and the conference was packed to the brim in anticipation of the arrival of these travellers from outer space.

In a blinding flash, and to the gasps from everyone in the room, Simon and his contingent of security guards materialized in the middle of the room before their very eyes.

Simon turned to the world leaders and walked up to the microphone that had been provided for him and began to speak:

"Greetings, and thankyou to everyone attending this crucial gathering today. First, my apologies to everyone for the swiftness that this meeting was put on you. As an opening gift, I will be beaming down translator devices, so that there is no confusion in what is said between us. You just need to put them in your ears, just like a Bluetooth headphone. I will be answering your questions at the end of my address to you, as I'm sure you will have many."

A package was then beamed down to the conference room, and once the translators had been distributed amongst the many delegates, Simon began. He initially gave them a brief history on the concept of the nine colonies, telling them that the eighth colony of humans had already been all but wiped out through an intergalactic war.

He then went on to tell them about several of the other colonies, including the Mycien and Gozian races, and the confrontation with the Lunarians. He explained the ongoing slave trade that had been going on for some time with people being regularly abducted from Earth, albeit on a small scale. He also explained that he and many others had been rebelling against this with the help of other more friendly colonies, but that the situation had taken a turn for the worse with the involvement of the Katari, who were a vicious reptilian race with extremely advanced weaponry and ambition. He went on to tell them of their intentions to invade Earth and about their alliance with the Gozians and Mycien.

He explained about the virus that had swept through the colonies that had made them infertile, and the discovery of a possible cure at the expense of human life on a mass scale.

Recordings of the battle between Lunaria and the Gozians had been downloaded onto playable data sticks, including the coded message from George explaining the outcome of the katarians last meeting with general kulos.

Simon then made it clear that in approximately four- or five-months' time, give or take, the invasion would begin, and unless they could unite and prepare defences, all human life would be either taken for scientific experiments, used for food and slavery, or exterminated and the planet would be stripped of all assets, making it inert and uninhabitable.

He explained that he had brought his fleet of ships and certain technology to help them, but that this was going to be a life-changing event on a grand scale. No matter what the outcome, the odds were most definitely stacked against them.

Once he had stopped talking, he was inundated with questions from all races and not everyone was totally convinced by his claims. A mixture of shock and panic could be felt throughout the room.

Simon answered as many questions as he could and then declared a recess so that they could discuss his proposition in his absence. He then gave the signal and beamed his party back to the Amelia, leaving them communication devices to notify him once they had come to a decision.

Once back on the Amelia, Simon headed back to his quarters, as he hadn't quite got over his solar ordeal yet and needed more rest.

Several hours passed by before the call came to say that Earth's leaders were ready to talk. After getting himself together, Simon made his way to the bridge, where he found Elle waiting for him.

"Hey Elle, back already? "Said Simon as he hugged her. "That was a short visit; you must have missed me pretty badly."

"Well, someone has to look out for you. And you've certainly made your presence felt here on Earth. You definitely don't do things by half, do you?"

"What do you mean?" asked Simon.

"Well, it's a media circus out there, and you have most of the world leaders at your beck and call. The population below us don't know whether to celebrate our arrival or panic at the reason for our arrival, and so far, no one seems to know what's going on."

"And that's the way it'll stay, until we've agreed the way forward. And talking of that, I must go and address that right now. There is one thing you could do for me though."

"What's that?" she asked.

"Well, we've established a link at the Stonehenge transport device, but we're not sure where it leads and how inhabitable it will be when you get there, so can you take a team and investigate that for me, please?"

"Of course, sweetheart. No problem," she replied

"Anyway, how did your visit go?" asked Simon.

"Well, I just told everyone that I was on a tour of duty, I didn't mention the fact that I'd been living in another galaxy in case they thought I was crazy. Although I might as well have told them, as your presence here confirms that anyway," said Elle laughing.

Simon went onto explain what had been going on at the conference, and the fact that he was about to get their response. In the meantime, Stonehenge had now been activated and they were ready to send a team through to the other side. They had confirmed with probes that it was a breathable atmosphere, but very little else. Elle wasted no time in volunteering to lead the team through the device; in fact, she was quite excited to see what was on the other side.

Simon kissed Elle on the cheek, and after a short rest, he headed down to the transporter bay and beamed back down to the conference room for round two with the politicians.

To his surprise, they seemed to have made a fair bit of progress, with most leaders now in agreement to look at and contribute to a plan of action. There had been quite a bit of debate about who would take the lead and run the show from Earth.

USA, China, Russia, and the United Kingdom had formed and headed up a sort of temporary alliance with the Arab and African nations also on board. Make no mistake, it would take a worldwide effort from all the world leaders to help build defences and to supply scientists, engineers, and general manpower.

USA agreed to use NASA and all its facility's and to fully cooperate with the Russian equivalent Roscosmos.

There were a few leaders that took the view that they didn't believe what they had been told and did not trust Simon, so they would not be contributing, but the negative voices were few and far between.

Now that they had found some consensus, Simon agreed to supply them with the specifications on how to build a planetary defence system, which he would power up for them once it had been installed.

They would also build an attack station which would be sited on the moon, and retro fit the space station with weapons and shielding. Initially they would have the element of surprise, but that wouldn't last for long with the fire power that they'd be up against.

There wouldn't be enough time to build massive spaceships, but Simon did include blueprints to retrofit existing jets into smaller orbital attack craft.

It was also pretty obvious to everyone concerned, that this wasn't something that they could keep out of the press, so they decided to arrange a meeting with representatives of the world's media and the four main leaders, with a question-and answer set-up. They would give a basic outline of what was heading their way and assure the press that Simon and his friends were not enemies of Earth, but were here to assist in protecting them.

As Simon beamed back onto the ship he was greeted once again by Elle who led him to the conference room to discuss what she had discovered.

The good news was that the planetary transporter was working fine, even better than expected. And it was linked to a planet at the far end of the galaxy which was indeed habitable. In fact, at first glance there was evidence that a primitive lifeform had lived there before, although there was no sign of them now.

It was very tropical in looks and temperature, and the air quality was extremely good. On top of everything else there was also a thriving animal population and, of course the most important thing, an adequate supply of water.

All in all, it seemed that it exceeded all their expectations.

The downside was that there was no technology or modern infrastructure of any kind, other than the alter stones and planetary transport device. To make the planet useful, they would need to transport technology, tools, and machinery on a grand scale, not to mention the labour force that would be required.

"Ok, I'll arrange a meeting with the fantastic four to work out the logistics of it all. And I think well name the planet Selene after the Greek goddess of the moon as a tribute to Princess Helaine. After all, we wouldn't be here now if not for her help."

"Nice; I like that. But who are the fantastic four?" asked Elle.

Simon laughed. "I mean the alliance that's been agreed upon between Russia, USA, the UK, and China. sorry I always hand out sarcastic nicknames. It helps me remember who I'm dealing with."

"You could invite them up to the Amelia as a good will gesture and afterward arrange for them to visit the Amazon rain forest," replied Elle, smiling.

"Ha-ha, I see what you did there," said Simon, "but I think I'll stick to Selene. But that's actually not a bad idea; I'll get on to it right away."

Simons crew contacted the fantastic four, and they had no hesitation in accepting the offer. They were all very eager to see the Amelia, and of course to visit the planet, Selene. They also requested permission to bring their own scientists and advisers, which Simon agreed to.

Elle and Chris headed back with their team to the Stonehenge site to see if they could expand the transport circle to make it feasible to move larger machinery, materials and of course large groups of people.

Simon agreed to give them forty-eight-hours to assemble their teams, and a meeting was set up to brief the press.

The next two days went by quickly, and before he knew it the delegates started arriving, and Simon began shaking hands with the world leaders and their teams. This was a momentous day and a long way from where his story began.

After the grand tour of the ship, they all beamed down to the Stonehenge site. Several of the press hierarchy were also invited to keep the positive media in line and on side in a move to reassure the public, and to stop them going into panic mode.

As they arrived, they were greeted by Elle and Chris who briefed them on the side effects of brief nausea and dizziness that came from planetary travel.

"So, is everyone ready?" asked Elle

The response was unanimous, and the excitement was clear to see on all their faces.

"Ok then, when you're ready Elle," said Simon.

"Oh, and we've managed to expand the transporter range," said Elle, "so we can now transport larger groups and machinery et cetera. ...OK, stand by, everyone, and prepare to be dazzled!" As she activated the device.

In a flash of light, they dematerialised and seconds later arrived on Selene.

It took a moment for everyone to refocus, but when they did, they were amazed at what lay before them.

They were now standing on a carpet of soft foliage inside a circle of stones similar to where they'd just come from. Surrounding the circle of stones were knee high fernlike plants leading up to tall trees covered in red and green foliage that glistened in the sunlight. The sound of creatures filled the air, and the heat was intense, but a cool breeze blew through which was actually reminiscent of the Amazon rain forest.

Elle's team had already scoped out the area in advance using drones and had discovered freshwater rivers in every direction.

Each group split up and headed off with one of Elle's team members acting as a guide in different directions. They spent most of the day on the planet exploring their designated areas and taking samples off the land from the ground and of course the water and from the fruit hanging from the trees, and then returned the to transport site for their journey back to Earth.

The general feeling about the trip was excitement and exhilaration and over the next few days, they each agreed to take a point of the compass to make their own.

Materials, machinery, and of course a labour force were transported to Selene to begin creating refugee camps and an infrastructure for them to be able to receive their own groups of people in the future.

It was obviously going to be a huge undertaking, and each of the fantastic four aligned themselves with blocks of other countries to assist in this mission.

The job of moving, managing and organising this project was given to Elle and Chris, and an arrival centre and medical camp would also be built around the transport area which would be headed up by Sabrina and her team, as there would no doubt be injuries for an operation of this scale.

Simon was working with different teams all over the globe to produce the orbital defence beacons, as well as weapons for handheld use and of course arranging a plan of action for the eventual evacuation.

The world's population had now been apprised of the reality of the war that was heading their way, by the press and the media, and in general they were doing it in a positive way, emphasising the points about the evacuation to Selene and the fact that Simon and his armada of ships were there to help protect them.

Martial law and curfews were enacted throughout the world as a precaution to stop potential looting, rioting, and any other criminal activity.

Over the next few months, with most countries united in the joint cause, a tremendous amount of work was achieved.

Europe, Saudi Arabia, and India naturally aligned themselves with the United Kingdom, while China sided with Asia.

USA joined with Australia, Cuba, Mexico, and Israel, while Russia joined with most of the eastern block and the Baltics.

Between all these alliances they'd managed to construct almost 60 per cent of the defence beacons that would be required to encircle the planet and, with Simon's help, were well on the way to installing them.

The planet Selene was also being developed at a rapid pace, with four zones now clearly set up. A huge workforce had already been relocated there with their families, and the first satellite had now been launched into space which gave them greater communication abilities as well as GPS and broadcasting. Work was commencing on a sewerage system and a network of pipes to supply safe drinking water.

Each of the four zones had their own military and security contractors, and with Sabrina's help, medical sites had been set up in all the four zones.

Things were moving at an incredible pace.

Back on earth there was now an establish lottery system for women under thirty years old and children to enter with thousands of people each week wining the right to travel to the planet Selene to avoid the impending conflict on Earth.

Still many people over the age of thirty were extremely frightened and unhappy about being excluded from the initial migration.

In most countries there was a massive influx of applications to join the armed forces, which would undoubtedly boost defences all over the world, and many countries introduced compulsory conscription into the armed forces to train and teach people how to use weapons and to boost defences globally.

The underground railway networks had been utilised and adapted to house those that weren't able to fight because of old age or disability.

Work had also been taking place in Earth's orbit, with the space station being retrofitted with a forcefield and weapons as well as reception pods and extra compartments so that the crews of the smaller attack craft, could get some rest and downtime away from their ships.

Simons attack craft defence systems were also upgraded, and finally remote-controlled anti-aircraft weapons from Lunaria that could destroy smaller space craft were installed on several of the smaller attack vessels.

* * *

Back on the Amelia, the alarms on the early warning system began to go off. It seemed that the invasion force was now appearing on the long-range sensors.

In response to this information, Simon called an emergency meeting with his lieutenants, small craft captains, and the four main leaders as well as selected press members.

The press and delegates began arriving along with representatives from Simon's fleet, and they quickly took their seats in the conference room.

The tension could be clearly felt in the room, and you could cut the atmosphere with a knife. A video link had been set up to include many of the world leaders.

Once everyone was seated, the conference began with Simon disclosing the fact that they had around eight weeks before the arrival of the Katari/Gozian fleet.

Many questions were then put to Simon regarding the incoming invasion force, for instance: How big was the approaching fleet? Would there be a ground invasion, and if so, where would this take place first? what cities would be targeted?

"I can't tell you how many ships are coming, "said Simon, "But after looking at our sensor array, it's safe to say that it is vast. As far as what cities will be targeted, I would imagine that most major cities will be hit simultaneously to cause as much disruption and confusion as possible, and yes, there will be a ground invasion all over the world,"

"So, what is the plan of action?" asked a member of the press.

"Firstly, and most important, for us to have any chance of success, we need to complete the planetary defence ring. Secondly, the evacuation to Selene needs to begin immediately, and thirdly, we need to accelerate the building program of weapons and the smaller attack craft that Russia and the USA are building as we speak. Then we wait and defend this earth with all our lives."

Many more questions were thrown across the room, and as

many that could be answered were addressed.

Once the meeting was concluded the delegates returned to Earth, and began to enact a plan of action, starting with the evacuation to Selene.

Assembly points around the world were announced and fortified. Military transport was mobilised to collect the lottery winners, selected leaders, and dignitaries.

The Amelia and several of Simon's fleet positioned themselves in orbit around the globe to transport people from the holding camps to the Stonehenge site, which was now a no-go area for a five-mile radius and protected by a ring of armed forces.

The mobilisation of the older generation and disabled began, and the underground stations began filling up fast.

Over the next two months, they managed to complete the defence ring around the planet, which was then charged with solar fusion by Simon. Then, through a tremendous amount of work and urgency, they were actually able to produce another thirty smaller attack crafts which were launched into orbit to join the rest of the fleet.

The invasion force was now only a couple of days away, and they could see that it comprised of at least three Katari master ships, and a couple of hundred smaller craft which were probably a mixture of Mycien and Gozian vessels.

Behind these were several medium sized cruisers.

There was no attempt to disguise the size of their fleet, as they obviously had no fear of any resistance that Earth would be able to mount. This was Simon's element of surprise, although it wouldn't last long, and as soon as the defence beacons were activated, it would quickly become apparent to the incoming attack force that Lunarian technology was present around the Earth. For them to use this advantage, they would need to make the first strike!

While the mobilisation of troops and the evacuation progressed on the ground, Simon and several of his fleet took strategic positions around the international space station and cloaked their vessels to lay in wait.

15

The Final Conflict

As an extra precaution, hundreds of magnetic mines had also been placed in orbit around the space station, waiting to be activated, and a worldwide warning went out for everyone remaining on the earth to either take up their positions or to stay indoors.

As the invasion fleet approached the earth's moon, it came into full visual range of the Amelia's advanced sensor array.

They were now only a quarter million miles away, and with the engine technology that they possessed, it would only take about twelve hours to arrive within striking distance.

At this point in time the invading fleet still had no idea of the presence of Simon's fleet and the defence ring around the earth. Normally they would already be scanning the area for other vessels, but through their arrogance and over confidence they didn't bother.

The order for radio silence was strictly observed, and as they approached the international space station, they settled into a matching orbit.

This was Simon's chance; it was now or never. As the enemy fleet drew within range, a coded signal was sent out, and the Amelia, followed by several smaller vessels, simultaneously decloaked and began their attack run towards the leading Katari master ship. They hit it multiple times with drone missiles and Lunarian solar weapons. Simon targeted their engineering section, while the other ships hit the shield generators and the helm.

The Katari vessel took massive damaged from the unexpected attack before managing to raise what was left of its shields. But the attacks kept coming, constantly wearing down their defence system. Within a few minutes, though, hundreds of smaller Gozian, Katari and Mycien vessels were dispatched and began to engage Simon's first wave. Very soon it was clear that their attack was no longer tenable, as they were being hit from all directions, forcing them to turn tail and run towards Earth.

The invading fleet pursued them vigorously and destroyed the smaller crafts that had accompanied the Amelia. They were outnumbered and outgunned, and as the Amelia entered a lower orbit, Simon activated the mines around the space station, and the defence ring which lit up like a carousel around the planet.

The magnetic mines instantly locked onto the damaged Katari vessel, and explosions began occurring all over the already weakened hull, destroying what was left of its shield generators. Simon then played the last ace up his sleeve as the weapons on the space station began blasting holes in the helm and engineering sections, crippling their engines and destroying the command centre. The invading fleet naturally turned its attack on the space station, and with their fire power, it didn't take too long to penetrate its shields and obliterate it into millions of pieces. But the damage to the Katari master ship was obvious as it burned and drifted aimlessly out of control.

Several of the Gozian vessels that had chased the Amelia to Earth, penetrated the defence ring before it had been fully activated and put up a bit of a fight. But this didn't last, as the rest of Simons fleet were lying in wait and quickly dispatched them.

The defence ring went into attack mode, and after destroying multiple craft and damaging many more, the remaining vessels quickly turned tail and returned to a safe distance with the rest of their fleet.

First victory had gone to Simon, and the airways were now full of voices cheering and screaming shouts of defiance to the invading fleet. Simon joined them in their celebration, but in his heart, he knew that this was only the beginning. The battle for Earth was far from over, and the enemy's response would be severe. Simon also knew that the attack on the Katari vessel, would have serious repercussions. But as he saw it, they were intent on destroying the earth without any concern for the population anyway. Why else would they raise an army and travel across the galaxy.

An hour passed by without any further incidents, and then the uneasy calm was shattered by an extremely noisy frequency burst which instantly knocked out all of the earth's satellites. The invading army then split into two, leaving half their fleet stationed just out of range of the defence ring. The other half, led by one of the two remaining Katari ships, headed to the other side of the planet.

Once in position they began scanning the defence ring from both sides of the planet.

"Ok, everyone be on your guard!" said Simon to his fleet. "They are scanning for weaknesses in the forcefield. I don't think they'll find anything, and that will leave them no option but to start a concentrated attack on the defence beacons."

"Sir, we have an incoming broadcast from the Katari vessel," said Simon's communications officer.

"Put it through," he replied.

A gravelly yet familiar voice came across the airways:

"Well, well ... congratulations on your opening gambit. I must admit that no one here saw that coming. But I am glad that you are here. Now I'll have the pleasure of torturing and killing you myself, just like I did with your friend George, only he's still alive, if you can call it living. He's in my brig being tortured as we speak, screaming and begging for his life."

"General kulos, if I die protecting my planet, then I die with pride and honour, as will George. Unlike yourself, who will die here as a Katari lapdog and a coward, because that's all a murdering bastard like you is worth. So, bring it on! We're not scared of you, and you'll find that defeating this planet won't be the push over your expecting."

"You will die, and your people will be enslaved or killed." replied general kulos angrily.

"Bring it on, you tosser. We'll be ready for you."

* * *

On the earth's surface a massive operation was taking place to evacuate as many people as possible to the planet Selene.

Elle and Chris's team had been working flat out, transporting as many of the population and supplies as they possibly could, and had now managed to move millions of people to their new destination, and although the satellites that orbited Earth had been knocked out, they were still in constant contact with the Amelia using the Lunarian communication devices and therefore would know exactly when it was time to pull the plug on the operation. As an extra precaution, shield generators had been placed around the Stonehenge area, masking the operation from space.

The rest bite in orbit didn't last long, and as predicted, the attack on the defence ring began from both sides of the planet. The Gozian cruisers along with the Katari master ships attacked the beacons with long-range weapons, so as to keep out of retaliation range.

As the beacons couldn't lock on to anything, they automatically switched all their power to the defence grid to strengthen the forcefield.

Simon knew that with this kind of fire power, it was only a matter of time before they began to fail. So he ordered his fleet to split into two to prepare for the eventual break through.

Sure enough, after a couple of hours of constant pounding, the targeted beacons began to fail.

"Ok, they're about to punch a couple of holes in the forcefield," Simon announced. "Once this happens, the smaller craft will penetrate the defence ring. With that in mind, I think it's time to switch it to all-out attack mode, as that will cause some damage to the incoming vessels and stop the larger ships from immediately entering orbit around Earth."

The first beacon failed, and as predicted, the first ships to push through were the Mycien vessels. Several of them took direct hits and were instantly destroyed, but the volume of vessels coming through was enough to ensure that many of them did make it. They instantly turned and fired on the defence beacons from inside the ring where its defences were much weaker.

Minutes later the beacon on the other side of the planet failed and they followed the same procedure. Simons fleet immediately engaged in battle with them destroying many of them, but not before the whole defence grid collapsed under the weight of the attack.

At this point the rest of the armada moved into attack Simon's vessels. They put up a brave fight, but within an hour of heavy fighting Simon had lost half of his fleet, with many other ships heavily damaged. On the bright side, they had managed to destroy at least a third of the incoming fleet and of course destroyed one of the Katari master ships. This was probable the best he could hope for.

The remaining vessels now turned their full attention to the Amelia, which had itself already taken heavy damage. Its shields were down to a minimum and there were hull breaches right across the ship. It was time to abandon ship, before the Amelia was either destroyed or boarded. Capturing Simon would be a serious blow to the moral of his men as well as the forces and leaders of the earth's continents.

Simon ordered the ships computer systems to be locked down and encoded and set timers for the engineering and power grid to shut off, he then gave the order to abandon ship and for the remaining vessels to retreat to fight another day.

Once this was done, Simon beamed down to Kelvedon hatch near Brentwood in Essex, England. Here he entered a secret subterranean nuclear bunker that had been used during the cold war in the 1950s. it had now been repurposed to house the prime minister and the armed forces operations centre for the battles that lay ahead. A Lunarian defence system had been installed around the bunker to mask its existence, as well as a radar system and sensor array that didn't rely on satellites so that they could track the movements of the invading ships and troops on the ground.

Similar set-ups had been installed in America, China, and Russia.

Simons first orders were to Elle to shut down the Stonehenge operation immediately before they were discovered.

They had already stopped receiving evacuees for some time now as they knew that the clock was ticking, and they were desperately trying to clear the massive backlog of people waiting to transfer to Selene.

Unfortunately for some, time had now run out. Anyone that didn't make the transfer deadline was now escorted to the prebuilt holding bunkers that had been built to house them while they were waiting.

This obviously caused a lot of anger, resentment, and hysteria. This was dealt with by the armed forces channelling any protesters by force into the bunkers.

Once this was achieved, Elle sent Chris and Sabrina through the portal, closed it down, and then beamed over the bunker to join Simon and his team.

It wasn't long before the attack on the planet earth began.

Shuttle crafts began appearing all over the world, and the larger vessels that had positioned themselves in orbit began bombarding the cities with pulse cannons and energy weapons. The shuttles also began firing on the towns and cities.

The militaries of the world instantly engaged them with fighter jets but were outpowered and out gunned and were a lot less manoeuvrable than the advanced vessels that they were fighting. Although they did have some success in destroying various ships, it came at a cost, with the loss of jets at a ratio of about five to one.

It was clear they were not going to be able to sustain these kinds of losses for very long. The ground forces were also able to take out a few of the shuttles with surface to air missiles, but once pinpointed, they were immediately attacked and destroyed.

At this rate the planet would be conquered within hours, so plan B was put into action.

The power houses of the world had arranged a joint tactical strike, using multiple strategic nuclear weapons, which they had targeted at the two points in orbit that were housing the invading fleet.

The countdown began, and all the nukes were fired simultaneously for maximum effect.

As the weapons broke through the atmosphere several of them were targeted and destroyed, but many of them did reach their targets.

Silence fell across the room as it did with all the crises rooms around the world. The tension and anticipation could be clearly felt as they waited with bated breath to see the effects of the massive blast in orbit.

"Well?" the UK Prime minister asked, "Can you tell us if we've succeeded yet?"

As the sensor array settled, it soon became clear to everyone that the invading armada was still there. The only good news that Simon could give them was that many of the smaller Mycien & Gozian vessels had taken quite a hit and suffered damage as a result of the blast.

The bombardment of earth intensified at a frantic place, and towns and cities were quickly reduced to rubble. This continued for the next few hours ... and then, as quickly as it began, the bombardment suddenly stopped.

Reports began coming in from all over the globe of the remaining shuttles heading up into the atmosphere and leaving the earth's orbit.

"What's going on? Is it all over? Have they given up?" These were some of the many questions put to Simon as he confirmed with the help of the sensor array that this was actually happening.

"I'm guessing that they are preparing for the invasion of the ground troops," replied Simon

A coded message was sent out across the world to prepare everyone for what was to come and to take up defensive positions in readiness.

After a two-hour lull, reports started coming in of troops appearing from no wear on the outskirts of all the major cities. Once again, the shuttles re-appeared, this time in support of the troops on the ground.

The invading army began advancing and rounding up any surviving humans.

Many of the shuttles then began to land to unload military hardware before loading up with any humans they'd come across and captured.

As Simon looked at the sensor array, he quickly realized that as the shuttles landed, they dropped their forcefield while unloading. This was the first mistake; their overconfidence was clear to see and would cost them dearly.

After a flurry of messages across the world, the military units took full advantage of this and activated weaponised drones that had been stockpiled for an event just like this. As a result of this action, they managed to destroy dozens of vessels on the ground all at once.

Also, a resistance from both men and women had begun to form, and they were taking up arms supplied by the military forces around the world.

As the invading ground troops advanced through the rubble of what was left of the towns and cities, they were met with heavy resistance. Many of the earth's forces were equipped with Lunarian technology, and unlike the invaders, they knew the ground layout and were extremely successful in pushing back any advancing soldiers. For the first time for many of the invading troops, they were experiencing great losses, and fear and hesitation began to creep into their ranks. They had totally underestimated the humans' ability to defend themselves and their inbuilt attitude of 'Never Give Up and Never Surrender!'

Thanks to their coded message system, this action was repeated in all the bigger countries across the globe.

Unfortunately, though, there were the exceptions with many of the smaller islands and poorer countries, like Somalia and Africa didn't fare so well.

After hours of intensive fighting, with little ground gained or lost and with many lives lost or captured from both sides, the Decision was taken by the joint leaders to execute all prisoners, especially Gozians, as they were beginning to use their ability to get into the heads of their captives and turn them against their own kind. This decision wasn't taken lightly, but after many reports of mass open air executions of captured soldiers or anyone caught resisting against their invasion, it was the obvious response to send a message back to them that we could be just as ruthless.

After several hours of this stand-off, most of the invading armies began to withdraw and beam back to the ships they came from.

Once again, the questions began to fly, but they were soon answered, as the bombardment on the ruined cities began again in an attempt to destroy the entrenched troops that were protecting them. This was a very negative tactic, as they had come here to capture as many humans as possible and to take any resources they could lay their hands on.

The renewed bombardment of the planet was intensified and having a devastating effect on the ground. Many lives were being lost as a result of this.

Suddenly and without warning the attack on Earth stopped, and the night sky was filled with light, and loud crashing noises like thunderclaps.

On the sensor array it was clear that the invading army had either doubled in size, or they had just been joined by an opposing force. Judging by the noise and fireworks above them, it appeared that the latter was true.

"Mobilise the remainder of our ships," said Simon to Elle. "I need to get up there and see what's going on."

Simon then spoke to the UK prime minister and informed him of his plans to leave orbit, leaving him in charge of the sensor array equipment.

Elle contacted the remaining captains who were protecting the underground bunker and gave the order to re-launch their vessels and transport Simon and herself on board.

Once up in orbit, he was witness to the sight of Lunarian battle cruisers that were accompanied by a huge fleet of unidentified ships, that were engaging the Katari and Gozian vessels in battle.

The Mycien crafts were nowhere to be seen.

"Get me to the Amelia," Simon ordered. "I can contact them on their direct frequencies from there."

Simon's remaining entourage weaved their way through the battle zone, taking a few pot shots at the Katari ships in passing. Eventually they reached the war-torn Amelia, and after sending some reactivation codes through its systems, they were able to open the docking bay doors and enter the ship to land inside.

Simon and Elle quickly disembarked and headed to the bridge, where they unlocked the computer and immediately sent out a call to the Lunarian ships engaged in the battle.

After several seconds that seemed like hours to Simon, a warm and welcome voice came over the transmitter. "Hello, baby. Thought you might need some assistance."

It was of course his Princess.

Simon's eyes lit up, and a radiant smile spread across his face.

"What's going on? How are you here? and who are your friends? Not that I'm not grateful and extremely pleased to hear your voice."

"I couldn't lose the love of my life and would never forgive myself if I didn't help you. As far as my friends are concerned. I'm accompanied by the Kelisi fleet and the Osari.

I have been working with them to synthetically produce a vaccine to cure the infertile problem once and for all; in return they both agreed to help."

The Osarians were an ancient colony that now lived in huge man-made city like structures that have been constructed in orbit of their planet, which had become uninhabitable many years ago. The Gozians had recently cut off all trade with them over a financial dispute, and Helaine's people had convinced them that they might be next after Earth had fallen.

"I'm so excited to hear your voice too!"

"Oh My God!" replied Simon. "I love you so much. I just want to hold you in my arms and kiss you all over!"

"Well, they'll be plenty of time for that, but first we need to despatch these aggressors once and for all. The Myciens have already fled the scene, and the Gozian cruisers are heavily damaged and have now been cut off from any remaining troops on the ground."

It wasn't long before the smaller Gozian vessels were either destroyed or surrendered, and shortly after the destruction of one of the two remaining Katari ships, General Kulos's battle cruiser broadcasted a request for a ceasefire to discuss terms for surrender.

"Do you mind if I discuss terms with them?" asked Simon

"No not at all: be my guest. It was your tenacity and stubbornness that won this war. I just came to mop up for you," joked Helaine

"I think I've scratched your ship a little babe, any chance of sending over a repair crew or maybe give me a tow." said Simon, grinning in relief.

"Why don't you transport over to my ship and let me deal with your repairs? I can't wait to hold you in my arms and introduce you to the Osarians."

"I'd love too, but first I just need to talk surrender to this dickhead."

Simon took great pleasure in making the call to general kulos, telling him that if he personally surrendered into Lunarian custody to face a war crimes tribunal, then the remainder of his crew will be free to leave.

Any remaining troops on the ground will be rounded up and face justice at the hands of the earth's leaders. Also, all captured humans would need to be released immediately.

There were hundreds of Gozian troops on board Kulos's cruiser, and many more in smaller vessels, so against his better judgement, he had no choice but to surrender. And after what he did to Princess Helaine's parents, his chances of survival were slim to none.

Lunarian and Osari troops beamed over to general Kulos's flagship cruiser, and personally took control of the release of any prisoners on board as well as arresting and removing General kulos himself.

As they emptied the brig, they came across the individual cells, where they found Simon's old friend George, who was in a very poor state but still alive. Surprisingly, in another chamber they also came across Lieutenant Angel Charmers, who had been isolated from the crew, as she was indeed pregnant with George's human child, and they were still not sure of the repercussions of this act.

The Katari battled on briefly, but once the Lunarians had taken custody of general kulos, they knew it was a matter of time before the game was up. They were being attacked from all sides, and eventually, after taking heavy damage to their remaining vessel, they also agreed to a ceasefire and to release the captured humans they had on board in return for a passageway home. The terms of their surrender were agreed, and like the Gozian commander, the Katarian commander was also taken into Lunarian custody, and their vessel was disarmed before it was allowed to leave.

Simon transported over to the Aurora, where he held Helaine in his arms and kissed her over and over. He then went down on one knee and asked her to marry him ... and with great pleasure and glee, she of course said yes, many times over.

***

The battle for earth was over. Many lives had been lost, and towns and cities were destroyed, but it could have been much worse. Earths forces once again took control of their lands, capturing and incarcerating any remaining alien troops and technology.

Elle beamed back down to the Stonehenge site to reopen the gate and transported through to Selene to join Chris and Sabrina. There she let them know how the battle panned out and to inform them that it was now safe to return if they so wished. For the moment at least they decided to stay in this new world that they had created.

Simon had now become a legend on Earth amongst his own people, and those that followed him in distant galaxies. Helaine introduced Simon to the Osari commanders whom he thanked with all his heart. And for now, at least there was peace in the galaxy and amongst the colonies.

Still, the slave trade and many other issues remained to be resolved. Just one big step for mankind across the galaxy had been achieved today, which could potentially put an end to this negative practice. There would obviously be many more steps along the way to root out the evils of mankind across the colonies.

But for now, at least, the turmoil was over......

Printed in Great Britain
by Amazon